T0116361

III Chronicles

Darlene Klingensmith,

Chronicler

This Chronicler's life and experience is

Consecrated

to

The Prince of Peace

Jesus, The Christ

Order this book online at www.trafford.com
or email orders@trafford.com

Most Trafford titles are also available at major online book retailers.

Print information available on the last page.

ISBN: 978-1-4251-1400-8 (sc)

Trafford rev. 05/18/2015

 www.trafford.com
North America & international
toll-free: 1 888 232 4444 (USA & Canada)
fax: 812 355 4082

CONTENTS

Dedication and Giving Thanks

"For God so loved the world that he gave his only Son,
that whoever believes in him
should not perish but have eternal life.
For God sent the Son into the world,
not to condemn the world,
but that the world might be saved through him."

John 3:16-17

The Lord has sent many people into my life. Adults and especially children, one way, or another have all been a blessing to me.

Especially do I esteem the Lord sending into my life:

My faithful family.

The Rev. Dr. James Boos, a child of God, a follower of Jesus Christ. Jim lives Scripture and shares his Lord and Savior easily with others.

My Professors: University of Pittsburgh
                  Pittsburgh Theological Seminary

I am absolutely grateful to my friends and neighbors, countless pastors, elders, deacons, choir directors, choirs, educators, secretaries, my many editors, who have read and commented on my manuscript, and all others for their encouragement, support and care of me.

To my Lord. My life and what I am are entwined with Him, and my commitment to Him. I have tried to make my life worth the truth of His death. Because I know Jesus Christ, I know truth and it is His truth that has set me free. I know my worth because Jesus did accept me as I was and accepts me as I am. With wisdom, love and direction from Him, I have worked very hard in getting to know who I am and this is a process never finished. I keep trying.

And so should you.

PREFACE

I Chronicles 16:34

"O give thanks to the Lord,
for he is good;
for his steadfast love
endures forever!"

I and II Chronicles are Old Testament Books telling the history of God's inter-action with His people. My III Chronicle is simply a sharing of the Trinity's interaction, grace and guidance and is God's history with me. My wondrous life experience – past ~ present ~ and ~ future - has been given me through God's saving grace, His son Jesus Christ and in the power of the Holy Spirit.

During the past years, I have shared meaningful conversations with many peo-ple of all ages and particularly I've enjoyed speaking with the very young. Upon hearing of my interaction with the Trinity, most have said to me, "But He doesn't speak to me. God doesn't speak to me. Jesus doesn't speak to me. I have never heard His Voice! Why doesn't He speak to me?"

I then ask, "Do you take time to listen for His Voice? Or do you just jump up from prayer and go on your way? Are you ever still and take time to just listen for His Voice?" Few say they are still and take quiet time to listen.

Many with whom He speaks, tell me they are afraid to let anyone know they have heard His Voice. It becomes an inward locked secret. Why? Because they don't want to be considered by others as being weird, crazy or odd.

For those who hear His voice but are afraid to share their experience with oth-ers, it is my prayer that my experience will give them the freedom to speak and share God, Jesus Christ and the Holy Spirit in their interactions with others!

It is my hope that my Chronicle, my journey and my experience with the Lord will set you free to speak and be free to share the Words and Voice of the Lord as He speaks to you.

I have placed after each Scripture and at the end of each chapter, some space to write down any thoughts that may be a part of your Spiritual walk.

I pray our Lord's presence and His peace be with you as you answer His call for you to do His will in your life.

March 2007   Rev. Dr. Darlene Klingensmith, Retired
Whidbey Island, Washington

+ The Beginning +

"Now the word of the Lord came to me saying,
"Before I formed you in the womb I knew you,
and before you were born I consecrated you;'"

Jeremiah 1:4-5a

This is my Chronicle, my journey with God, His Son Jesus Christ and the Holy Spirit: The Trinity.

I have been blessed with many proofs in my life; supremely so by a loving, caring, compassionate Lord Creator. Do I believe the words of God found in Jeremiah? Yes, truly and passionately, I do believe!

I came into this aesthetically beautiful, extraordinary and wonderfully made world as a Western Pennsylvanian. I began life in the rolling hills in a village called Pleasant Hills near Pittsburgh. I am child number five of six children, with three brothers and two sisters.

We all were given nicknames very early in life. The first born was Sonny, next Sissy, Alfie, Moses, then me, Beanie, and Honeybee. We grew up supporting each other mostly by giggling or out right laughing with and at each other.

When I was nearly three years old, we moved into a huge old farmhouse in Monroeville, a small village, still near Pittsburgh. I remember clearly the kitchen and very small living room. There was a huge yard in which we ran, played games and climbed trees.

I believe it was here that my love and reverence for nature began, particularly for:

Trees and wildlife,
    Butterflies and eagles,
        Still waters and crashing waves,
            Mountains and grand canyons,
                Blue skies and sunshine,
                    Snow, rain and rainbows,
                        People and all life,
For everything God created.

To this moment, I can recall distinctly and very explicitly, my first encounter with God. My mind has retained this impeccably and I remember it as much as I can remember any event in my life, even those which have just happened. And yes, I was but three years old. The encounter began early one evening while my parents were at the grocery store. I was left with my brothers and sister and apparently I was looking for something to do. Sitting down on the floor, I began to play with a bottle of ink, uncorked the bottle, and spilled some of it on the heel of my foot. I tried to clean it off but couldn't. My brothers and sister began to make fun of me, telling me that ink was poison and that I was going to die.

I believed them.

I became very frightened, and even though I didn't have any "inkling" what death was, I hid in the darkened living room. I was unable to reach the light switch, and so I crawled up onto an overstuffed, velvety, scratchy-covered chair. I then declared to myself, that if I was going to die, I would do it alone and in the dark! I tried hiding by crouching as far as possible into the corner of the chair. I remember quietly sobbing, feeling utterly lonely and very frightened.

As I cowered in the dark, stomach churning and shivering from fright, there came into my mind's eye a vision. I saw myself standing in an oblong, gracefully marbled courtyard - no walls, on a sunny day with a blue sky and several fluffy white clouds.

I then saw a tall figure and moved toward it. The closer I came to it - or it to me - I first saw and then I knew it was A MAN. He looked so perfect, tall and elegant, stately and kingly - I felt no fear, I somehow KNEW this MAN to be my friend. He was standing on an ivory marble floor at the top of a marble stairway, a stairway of seven small steps. He was dressed in a long white shimmering (like the sun dancing on ocean waves), cascading robe. I stood on the marble floor below the steps, looking up at Him. He was so supreme and ideal. His long, just below the shoulder, flowing hair and beard were both white. This color of white was as pure as I have ever seen. It is almost like the color that happens when an atom is split but more pure, more clear somehow. It has a warmth to it and is a perfect color but does not harm the eyes. This white was unlike any white color I have ever seen, actually the color is indescribable for somehow, it also contained depth and a feeling of perfect love.

Somehow I knew this MAN to be the perfect, kind, loving, grandfather image. THE MAN moved His left hand slowly and tenderly toward me. His eyes were soft and smiling, and with a gentle, compassionate and soft voice, He said to me, "You won't die." Instantaneously, I felt infused by His comfort, love, and the overwhelming feeling of being very safe. THE MAN then left, but the sensation, the encompassing feeling so overwhelming to me, was one of being loved ~ with a security which has remained with me in my life.

I stayed in the dark, with what seemed like an eternity, waiting for my parents to return. Finally they came home. My mother found me, scolded me for spilling the ink and took me back into the light of the kitchen. She scrubbed as much of the ink off as possible, and then gruffly told me, "that I wasn't going to die, and to quit being so silly."

I was then sent to bed. I had no feeling of loneliness. I knew security and contentment and was very aware of feeling love and safety from THE MAN.

Thus ended the first chapter of my life with THE MAN, and I called Him "THE MAN" throughout my childhood and young adult years. I always thought of Him in capital letters, even before I could read and write! I also came to know that THE MAN was the image God used to come to this child simply to free me from my very deep fears.

Our family did not attend church, and to this day I do not know why my mother had us baptized shortly after I was born. The Rev. L. M. Bonner came to our home and baptized the five of us. It was a mystery to me, but in retrospect, I believe firmly that my life has been mightily blessed because of that particular Sacrament and function of the Church. Did the water have a magic which protected me? I believe not, but I do firmly believe it was the prayers and baptismal remembrances of Christ's baptism and of the Church members own faithfulness and prayers which supported me. The Holy Spirit of the Church is one in the Body of Christ and with baptism I became part of the Family of God!

2

+ Second Appearance +

*"In the fear of the Lord one has strong confidence,
and his children will have a refuge."*

Proverbs 14:26

During the next two years, several incidents occurred which I clearly and distinctly remember. Two are recalled here.

In my second encounter, I once again met THE MAN. Our family still lived in that same wonderful farmhouse. I was about five, and I had a favorite stuffed animal that had been placed on the mantle of our stove. It was an old style stove, the oven located beside the burners, high off the floor. Mother was at the door talking to an insurance man and after interrupting her several times, and getting no response, I became determined that I would get my stuffed animal.

I clambered up the gas pipe on the side that the burners were on and grasped onto the handle of a pan of boiling water. I started to fall. The water came splashing down over me and I screamed one long, loud, terrified scream.

Mother came running in, grabbed me, sat me down very hard on the table and ripped my clothing from me. In her anger and haste, and also I am sure some fear, a patch of my skin came off my shoulder as she tore off my blouse. After drying me off, she became even more angry with me for not waiting for her to get my animal and also for spilling the water. She gave me no comfort.

She then put a towel over me and fixed a place for me to sleep on the sofa and I found myself back in that very dark living room. And it remained dark, very dark. In that day, no matter the illness, the drapes were always drawn, letting in no light.

And again, I felt no comfort and was very frightened. I couldn't comprehend what I had done that was so wrong. On orders from our mother, it was mostly Sissy and Alfie, who kept me wrapped in wet and smelly, but healing salve dipped strips of cloth. Indeed, I have few scars because of their loving care of me. I remember Sissy reading stories to me and my other brothers bringing me toys and crayons as we often played together in that darkened room.

I can see in my mind's eye, a wondrous happening that first night. Scared and trying to be as brave as possible, trying not to cry, I finally closed my eyes. It was then that I saw THE MAN for the second time. He was standing in the same place, still tall and 'shimmeringly', elegantly dressed. This experience though, was a little different than the first time.

THE MAN did not speak, but very slowly and fluidly raised His hand, palm out, toward me. It appeared as though He was a little distance from me, but at the same time, He seemed able to touch me. His face and eyes were as loving, deep and as warm as I remembered from the first time, yet it was His eyes that locked into mine and instantly, I felt the same comfort, security and love. THE MAN and His Presence stayed with me throughout my confinement in that room. To this day, I am sure it was because of His love for me, His presence with me, that I suffered little physical or mental scarring.

I stayed in that darkened room for several weeks. I was then released. My first day outside is a great memory. I can still feel the warmth of the sun on my face as I ran out into the yard to play and that it was very healing.

My life after that became rather innocent. I liked farm life. It was great to walk and jump in weeds and grass that was taller than me. I liked eating green apples from our orchard. I recall one very lovely day, climbing up a small, dying apple tree to feed apples to a few pigs in a pen under one of the tree's branches. As became my usual custom in years to come, I skinned my knees and elbows and I also tore one side of my belt loose from my dress. I had fun climbing out on a limb and feeding those pigs, but then mother found me, and became very angry with me, mostly because of the dress, but also for climbing up trees.

I cannot recall how I descended from the tree, but that was the beginning of my becoming what was then known as a "tomboy." I never "got over" my love of climbing. Even to this day, hiking and climbing mountains are what I like to do best!

The next year we moved again. This house had three bedrooms so that there were three sisters in one and three brothers in another. It was here that I began my schooling. We lived about five blocks from our school. As I started school, out of necessity, ours was a family of hand-me-downs. We all were particularly careful with our school clothes because we knew someone else would be wearing them and I tried to become very careful about ripping belts from my dresses! I remember distinctly an incident about a new coat, the first new anything that I can remember. I think I only remember it because my first grade teacher made several nice comments about how pretty I looked in it. She was a wonderful first grade teacher, and her name was Mrs. Saucer. Her kindness made me feel good, and her teaching made me love books and a thirst for learning developed in me. I know that Mrs. Saucer is a perfect example of an outstanding teacher!

I remember no more communication with THE MAN, but throughout my growing years, I do remember seeing Him occasionally when I closed my eyes, especially when I felt lonely. Somehow though, He became different. THE MAN was now more like a shimmery white marble statue, always in that same warm ivory marble hall. But no matter, moving or statue-like, the security and the feeling of being loved and safe were still with me, still a part of me.

3

+ Yet A Child +

"The beginning of wisdom is this:
Get wisdom,
and whatever you get,
get insight."

Proverbs 4:7

Growing up in a family of six children, mostly isolated on the farm, we learned to play many games together. There was always a game of football, baseball, races, tag, bicycling and "Mother May I?" being played. Also, when we moved into a small town where movies were available, we would share popcorn almost every Saturday afternoon.

I continued my tomboy ways. I loved being adventurous, climbed when I could, played sports and liked softball, baseball and basketball with my brothers. I also enjoyed the sports that females were allowed to play in that day. I became quite competitive. I wanted to excel, to achieve, and I can never remember quitting or giving up until I had tried my very best. I became a good student during my school years; indeed I liked school very much even though I was very shy. I had some great teachers all along my journey to adulthood. I never realized, until I discovered I had dyslexia, why I had such difficulty in school with math and typing. However, I survived school beautifully!

I would say my childhood was fairly typical of that day. Perhaps that is true except for one real distinct event that became a scar upon my memory at about the age of ten. What happened is now termed child abuse. My mother was a child abuser, physical abuse. She would scream at us as she hit us and tell us what awful children we were.

Child abuse was not a subject that was discussed in the 1940's . And because it was not, I became a lonely and bewildered child as I think happens to all abused children. Little did I know at my age, that my brothers and sisters were also abused - much more severely than I.

For me it began one night when my mother came into our bedroom and woke us up. She tore my blanket from me and began hitting me with our father's belt. When any angry parent, who seems to have already rejected a child many times in the past, lashes out with an object - be it a wooden spoon, belt, wooden paddle, broom handle, a switch from a rose bush, or whatever else may be available to use, while hitting and screaming at the same time "that people will never like a child like you!" something occurs within the child. When you are hit time after time, often a determination in the inner self happens. This happened to me.

She stopped hitting me when my father came in and said to her, "You need to stop, you must really be tired, come on downstairs." She left with my father and went downstairs.

What happened? Both the screams and lashings are silently accepted as a reality - you are a bad child and deserve no better - or you become defiant.

In my case, after she left the room, I grabbed tightly onto my blanket and huddled under it. At the age of ten, I chose silent defiance. I remember clearly shouting silently to myself these words, "Yes, too, people will too like me!" while I actually stomped my foot into my mattress beneath my safe covering, my blanket.

In my determination, mostly unconscious and certainly not deliberate, I strove to acquire an outgoing personality, but in reality I was quite shy, actually an introvert. I became an avid reader, and through my love of reading became excited about nature and poetry. Black Beauty by Anna Sewell became my favorite book. Rejection had caused one door to close but many others began to open. Many other people entered into my life with good influences especially my Junior and Senior High teachers. Their influence and care of me became strong and is still with me today. Mrs. Saucer, Ms. Brown and Mr. Hill are three that I remember distinctly along with many other outstanding teachers and people that I met on my life's journey.

Along my young life's path, it was for me questions, questions and more questions. Always asking myself,

"What did I do?
What is wrong with me?
Am I really a bad person?
Am I so ugly?
Why such rejection??

These questions are not easily answered and for me they were never answered. Neither have my sisters or brothers found any answers. And I will say that if you are not the one being hit, it seems worse for you than if it had been you. Love does that. We hurt for each other. None of us have ever understood our parents' behavior, we can only conjecture.

The phrase "an abused child makes an abusing parent" is quite true, generally speaking, but particularly in the case of my mother. It is my understanding that her childhood was filled with terror, loneliness, abuse and rejection. When my mother was born, there was no opportunity for hospital care. During birth, the best my grandmother could hope for was a midwife. The circumstance of my mother's birth is unclear. But the story is, when my grandmother went into labor she was alone at home, and only God knows for how long. When my grandfather came home, he was drunk and didn't realize what was happening and went to bed and slept.

The next day, when a neighbor came to check on my grandmother, she had bled to death.

My mother, along with her brother and sister were placed in an orphanage, and so with little chance of adoption, the pattern of life was repeated, that is with my mother but not my aunt and uncle. They were both adopted and mother blamed them for abandoning her. With education, love and reverence for life, I hasten to add that this pattern of abuse was broken in my siblings generation.

I thank God this ugly cycle was broken.

I tell about this abuse because it happened and caused my personality and life to begin to develop and be shaped. Mother was from the "old school" that thought the way to obedience was through physical punishment or perhaps my mother never knew what it was to be loved in her early years. We were from a German background, in which hugging and touching never happened. Never did I hear the words "I love you or you are a good child" from my mother. My father never said these words either, but I know from his touch and his kindness that he did love his children.

I have not put these events in writing to embarrass anyone, it is simply part of my life's journey.

Why do such events happen? I think and feel it is because God has graced us with the gift of freedom to decide our behavior and allowed each person to be free in their actions and reactions, not only toward each other but also to Him. God did not create us to be puppets. We are loved so much, God has graced us with free will.

My parents divorced many years ago and my mother died in 1992. It is my understanding that she never found any peace or happiness in her life. I fully hope that with death, she has found peace. Months before my dad died in 1987, he apologized for not interfering in mother's abuse of us. I believe that both my parents' childhoods heavily influenced their method, their behavior in rearing us children.

I worked very hard in school and I very much still like studying, despite being dyslexic. I graduated from Swissvale High School in 1952. I took commercial courses that seemed to have left me ill prepared for my ultimate future. I wanted to go to college and several of my teachers encouraged me, but mother said that college was only for boys and that girls only went to college long enough to meet someone and get married. I could not find financial help and there were no scholarships available, but it was always my dream to attend the University of Pittsburgh.

After graduation, I became a long distance telephone operator and two years later married and subsequently became the mother of three children, one daughter and two sons.

+ Sickness Comes +

"Cast your burden on the Lord,
and he will sustain you;"

Psalm 55:22a

Accidents happen and not always to some other family. One such incident happened to John, a lifelong friend, and a childhood neighbor. He had an accident that culminated in a malignant brain tumor. The brain surgery was not successful. The patient would not live. This "unsuccessful" surgery caused THE MAN to come into my life again.

I found myself sitting beside his hospital bed the day after the surgery and I said aloud, "IF there is a God, he is so young with so much more potential than me, please take me and let him live." More of a plea, it was just plain wishing on my part. However, those words barely escaped from my lips when a ray of sunshine came though the upper corner of the window in his room and lit on his head. I did a double take! I said to myself, "I must really be tired, WHAT WAS THAT?" I arose from the chair and went over to the window to look for myself. No sun.

I then walked across the hall to the lounge, I looked and found the sun to be on the other side of the building. I shook my head and said to myself, "You must really be tired, you really are seeing things!"

However, what I did see was ~ the University of Pittsburgh. I looked at it often during my visits. It was then that I made another plaintive plea - "Please, please, could I attend this Pitt University someday? PLEASE?"

Three days later, John was up and walking around and wanting to go home.

This appeared to be the third and last encounter with THE MAN, still I knew Him not.

Life once again fell into routine. In 1961, I took a Civil Service Exam and passed with an amazingly high score. Amazing because I actually guessed at most of the answers, or at least I thought I did. I then began to work in our small village, still near Pittsburgh, for the U. S Postal Service and worked there for twelve plus years; liking my work very much. Working at the Post Office was a learning, fun experience. I worked six days a week as a permanent temporary and opened the Post Office at six-thirty A.M each morning.

I was happy and content.
Still, there was something missing in my life. Fulfillment and purpose.

+ Gabriel? +

*"...And behold, there stood before me
one having the appearance of a man."*

Daniel 8:15b

For a brief time in my life, living and being alive was as perfect as it had ever been. My entire family, husband and children, were all healthy and content. We were all involved in some kind of sports, mostly baseball and I became a Little League manager for my oldest son's team and I really liked that job! It was mostly fun. My children were all doing very well in school. Life seemed so smooth, almost perfect.

In 1970, on one very pleasant day another encounter. The weather was perfect, sunny with a nice cool breeze. I was standing behind the counter, looking out the Post Office window. I was alone. The Postmaster, George, was at a meeting. My coworkers were at lunch or out delivering mail. I then asked myself, "Is this all there is to life?"

A voice answered and said, "No, there is much more." I looked around and saw no one; indeed I was quite alone. I looked in all the rooms, there was no one present.

Another year passed and George invited us all to his Presbyterian Church. Church?

A year later I became a member and began teaching Sunday School for the first graders. Another fun task.

It was here that I met another MAN but...
      I only met Jesus,
          The good Man
             The exceptional Man
                But not Jesus Christ , Savior.

However, I was very soon to meet The Christ. The first of a series of occurrences happened to me in the fall of 1971. This time in my life is also still vivid, profound and significant.

I was sleeping very soundly, yet awoke with the feeling that 'something' was in our house. I turned the light on, looked at the clock finding it was 2:00 AM. I looked around the room and hallway and saw nothing. I clicked the light off and closed my eyes, yet I still felt uncomfortable, very uneasy.

I opened them again, dark as it was, I saw a figure standing at the foot of the bed. It almost scared me to death. I was so frightened that I couldn't move, being able only to open and close my eyes. I kept opening and closing them thinking that I was dreaming, hoping that I was, wishing it to be, but every time I opened them, 'it' was still there. I have no idea how long this went on, only that I have never felt such terror and that it did seem like an eternity of time had passed by.

I was staring at a figure which appeared quite tall; 'it' seemed to be dressed in a black outfit with a hooded cape over it and had at one and the same time no definite sharp outline, yet an outline that I could see. The figure was not small, perhaps 6' 6" to 7' tall, with a muscular frame. It did not move or gesture. I could not see facial features. When it spoke, the voice seemed masculine and said, "I'll be back for you in a couple of years."

He stood for what seemed another long time while the words etched themselves into a place in my memory. His voice was powerful, with no trace of compassion, a steely monotone. The statement was blunt, strong, and positive. Then very fluidly, the figure backed into the hallway and was silently gone. The thought that went through my head was that I was going to die. I thought I had just been visited by death.

I laid there and listened as the door scraped against the floor as it was opened and again as it was being closed. I jumped up and turned on the outside lights, went out and saw nothing. Our Belgian Shepherd outside never stirred. But the next morning, my children wanted to know "what" was in the house during the night. It became known as "Mom's ghost friend" and was soon forgotten.

+ An Accidental Meeting +

"And Jesus said to them,
"Go into all the world
and
preach the gospel to the whole creation."

Mark 16:15

Through an innocent action, my earnest pilgrimage toward Jesus Christ began sometime in the summer of 1972. My family was outdoors when I went into the kitchen for a drink of water. Hearing the television on, I crossed the living room to shut if off. The Rev. Billy Graham was talking at the end of one of his crusades. He appeared to be looking into my living room, his voice clear. He said, "You there, in your homes, if there is something missing in your life, if you have everything but still are not completely content, then you need Jesus. Let Him give your life fulfillment. Won't you accept Jesus Christ into your life right now?" As I reached down to click off the television, I thought and said aloud, "Why not? What have I got to lose? Yes, Jesus come into my life!" Although sincerely said,

I hesitated,
    I waited, and —
        absolutely nothing happened — except ~
            I felt a tiny tingle for just an instant in my body.
I pushed the off button and went back outside into the summer.

Still, I knew Him NOT.

7

+ I Knew Him But Still Asked +

"And I tell you,
Ask,
and it will be given you;
seek,
and you will find;
knock,
and it will be opened to you"

Luke 11:9

On a lovely, Friday summer's eve in July 1993, my youngest son, Bill and I went to our county fair, especially to see a demolition derby. As much as we had looked forward to seeing the derby, right in the middle of it, I looked at my son, and I said, "Let's go home." He looked at me and said, "Yes, let's." We did not take out usual route, and upon arriving at home, found my other son, Rich waiting with sad news. There had been an automobile accident in which our uncle had been killed and my father was in critical condition. If we had come our usual route we would have seen my father's car. Better we had not.

My father and uncle were coming to visit us, and when he turned left to cross the highway, a woman came down the highway at very high speed, hit my father's car on the passenger side, hydroplaned over my father's car and landed in a yard, a perfect landing. She had turned to talk to one of the six children in the back seat and didn't remember what happened. The worst injuries from her car were two children with broken limbs.

Upon arriving at the hospital, we found our uncle had died shortly after arrival; all his bones had been broken, along with much damage to all his organs. My father was not expected to live; he had a bruised heart, broken ribs, ruptured spleen, punctured leg, kidneys not functioning and his heart rate, after being placed in intensive care, was barely showing movement on the monitor. He was cut from head to toe from the flying glass of the windshield as it shattered. Needless to say, both families were in a state of shock.

As we stumbled through Friday and Saturday, my stepmother felt the need for some spiritual comfort and asked if any of the ministers I knew would come to the hospital. Unknown to me, my stepmother was a Christian having been converted

26

at age twelve. Her sister, wife of the uncle who had been killed in the accident, was also Christian and both felt a deep spiritual need. I did not have this need, at least this is what I thought. Then on Monday, I talked with George and since all townspeople had post office boxes and visited daily, he suggested that he would ask the first minister he saw coming into the post office to come to the hospital and visit with us.

One did come. The Rev. James Boos. I met him in the hallway as I was leaving intensive care, knowing there was no hope for my father to live. His heart was barely beating, his kidneys stopped functioning, he was jaundiced and in a diabetic coma. He had not been diabetic before the accident and had been in very good health for a man of 71. I told the minister that my father was in a coma, but he suggested we pray for him anyway. The reason? Rev. Boos said that he would be talking to God and not my father.

We went into his room and although I knew that my father could not hear me, I still said to him, "Dad, there is a minister here, do you want a prayer?" My dad opened his eyes, looked at me, and said, "yes." He then closed his eyes and did not move. When I took his hand, it was cold and there was no response. Rev. Boos began to pray. I remember placing my right hand on my dad's arm and my left hand on his bed rail. I felt Rev. Boos' hand on top of mine. His hand, as he prayed felt extremely hot to me and I felt a strange surge of power go through me. I remember feeling both drained and exhilarated at the same moment. The prayer was short and to the point, "Please God, a return to good health if it be Your will through the name of Jesus Christ. Amen."

Two short hours later, his kidneys were functioning perfectly and my dad was eating Jell-O! He was out of the diabetic coma! I was in awe as I watched his heartbeat became stronger and stronger on the monitor.

Who was this God, and this Jesus Christ that Rev. Boos had talked to?

Yet, I knew Them NOT.

My uncle's funeral was, for me, one of the most bleak, black, saddest days of my life. My uncle just couldn't be dead! But he was. He had been too full of life. He was the brother my father never had and the adult friend that I never had. He was the first adult person who always greeted me and my family with a hug and sincere warm caring. When they placed him in the ground, I heard no words of comfort and my soul and mind were in deep, dark despair. What was the meaning of life and death? Was there any meaning to anything?

Summer and fall went along and my father improved daily and everything once again became very routine.

8

+ A Command - Lost +

"Jesus said to them, "Come and have breakfast."
Now none of the disciples dared ask him,
"Who are you?"
They knew it was the Lord."

John 21:12

During the first week of December, 1973, more than two years after my father's accident, a masculine Voice came to me in the middle of the night...
"Darlene, I command you to arise. Go and do as I command you."
The Voice was coming from outside the wall of the house, in through the bedroom wall.

I sat up in bed, turned on the light to make sure I wasn't dreaming, and I saw no one. I looked out the window, no one! I did not feel frightened, just disturbed. I did recall the "Ghost friend" that had visited me, but this Voice was very different.

I crawled back into bed, and again came the Voice, still outside the room. "I command you to arise!" I did not move this time, trying to figure out if I really was dreaming, even pinching myself, and by doing that I knew that I was VERY wide awake.

I was not frightened by the sound of the Voice because something in the tone or quality, although quite commanding, was gentle, loving, and kind. My emotions were under control; I was quite calm, feeling more peaceful than anything else.

Twice more the command came but these times the Voice was within the bedroom. Still I saw nothing, although the Voice seemed to penetrate the entire room. I then asked a most inane question in the middle of this happening - a simple "Why?"

No answer came. Nevertheless, the Voice was now inside my head. He said, "Go to a certain house, knock on the door. You tell the person who answers the door that you want to touch their son. You touch him on the right hand and he will be healed. He is in the front bedroom on the second floor."

I then asked, "Who are you?"

No reply came, just another, "I command you to go." I said, "You can heal him if you want to, you don't need me. Those people will think that I am nuts, at least crazy for sure."

And I did not go.

The six year old boy, whom I saw just once, died a few months later of leukemia. Subsequently, I realized how special this family was, all recognizing Christ as Savior, including the boy. One day, the grandfather came into the Post Office telling us about him. There were five other children in the family but he loved dearly, his first grandchild. His only wish was to hold his grandson once more before he died, but the child was in so much pain that he couldn't stand to be touched, even gently. The grandfather never held his grandson, but said that one day, he would be able to hold him on his lap, and that place would be ~ heaven.

To this day, there is a suffering in my soul for my disobedience, but
Still, I knew Him not.

Just WHO was this VOICE? I turned off the light, convinced myself that I had been dreaming - and besides, it was very cold outside. Yet deep inside, there is a point that is beyond reasoning and logic and I really knew the incident had been no dream...that Voice had too much power...too much authority...it was too disturbing to my mind and Spirit. I have never heard another Voice like it.

I quickly pushed this incident into the subconscious part of my mind - forgetting about it as soon as possible - post haste! The child, however, I have never been able to forget; every time I hear of someone with leukemia, I think of him.

9

9

+ A Unique Happening - My First Christmas +

"for to you is born this day in the city of David
a Savior,
who is Christ the Lord."

Luke 2:11

On December 24, 1973, I was standing at the counter in the Post Office, when Rev. Boos came in to get a package. He inquired about my father and we talked a bit about how great he was progressing. As he picked up his mail and was leaving, he said, "Merry Christmas." He hesitated a moment and then left.

I looked at the clock and it was 10:18 AM.

He later told me that he knew something had happened to me but didn't know just what, but that I looked as if I had been struck.

What happened was this - when he said, "Merry Christmas" I suddenly saw a cloak, not unlike the one on the stranger - my 'Ghost friend' - but it was royal red, covering him and at its top was a white dove trying to fly. It seemed unable to set itself free from around the cloak. I saw this for a mere instant. I drew back when I saw the cloak and dove, when just as suddenly something struck me, going from the top of my head and down through my entire body. When it hit me, I was knocked away from the counter several feet. I think that what I saw shocked me more than what I felt.

This was not the first time that I have seen something out of the ordinary, but was the first time to see an entire person in a color within such a confined space as a cloak. I had always seen color around certain people, not everyone, but had never seen anything like this before. I certainly did not understand what I had seen or felt. I only knew for sure that it put my mind into a mass of confusion. I was not frightened nor anxious, just terribly confused. I passed it off as daydreaming or just "another one of those things" that seemed to be happening to me more frequently ~ lately.

A co-worker, the previous week, had asked me to bring my family to her church for the Christmas Eve Candlelight Service and since we didn't go anywhere else at that time, she made me promise that I would come. When I realized that 'he - Rev. Boos' was her pastor, I tried desperately to think up some excuse not to go. Later on in the day, she had her husband make a special trip to see me to remind me to come to their church. I bless her to this day for insisting and persisting in

0

my coming to that service.

My children and I went to the service. I cannot remember everything that happened but I was most uneasy of mind by the time we entered the church. I do remember arriving later than we had planned and being forced to sit in the front - it is just NOT Presbyterian to sit up front!

As the service progressed, I felt strangely drawn to the pastor as he read the Christmas Scripture. I didn't hear the Scripture, but 'felt' it; for me it was words that were alive. I was in the City of Bethlehem! It was a strange, illuminating, wondrous sensation.

This feeling of hearing but also living in the Scripture was to stay with me throughout my conversion experience and beyond. My attention, indeed, my whole being was caught up in his reading of Scripture and in his sermon but I felt that his voice was being aimed right at me! For the first time in my life, I understood what Christmas was about - it wasn't just another 'good and perfect' baby being born, nor was it a holiday brought about by a commercial world to see how much profit could be made. The thought that this surely must be some sort of a special birth, God come to earth, kept my mind fully occupied.

But, something even more strange was about to happen. As I was sitting there wondering what was happening within me, it came time for The Lord's Supper. It was perhaps one of the most physical things to occur to me in the next four months. As the plate was passed, I took a Communion cup and was holding it, not paying much attention, when I suddenly realized my hand felt wet.

I looked down at it and could not believe what I was seeing! The cup that I had received, the plastic disposable kind, had a hole in the side near the top, and just as suddenly, I realized the grape juice was actually going up to the hole and down the outside of the cup, the juice resting in the palm of my hand. I showed it to my daughter, who was sitting beside me, and we both began to quietly giggle. I didn't know what else to do, so I put a tissue under the cup and drank the few drops that were left in it.

However by this time, I couldn't wait to get outside and get back to my home and get some rest! Surely that was all I needed!

Tuesday, Christmas Day was one of the most confusing days that I have ever experience. My mind was still in a whirl and at the same time I felt numb. Yet I was functioning in a perfectly normal manner, as I would do in the months that followed, but for this day, I realized that I was not thinking very clearly. I seemed unable to get my thoughts to function together. I also realized that the only time that my mind seemed clear and functioning had been in church the night before. This 'condition' of clarity would be with me for my entire conversion experience.

My son had gotten a stereo set for a gift. It had a set of earphones and I tried to use them to keep from thinking, trying to shut everything else out, but to no avail. I then began to have an emotional problem. Just what was the matter with me?

On Thursday, THAT pastor came into the Post Office and we all had a good laugh over the 'leaking' Communion cup. But that was not really why I had wanted to talk with him and I had sent him a note saying that I had a problem, but did want to try to think about it a little longer.

Rev. Boos phoned my home Saturday morning and said that he would be in his office and for me to come up and talk with him that evening.

+ Gifts +

"Blessed are the poor in spirit,
for theirs is the kingdom of heaven."

Matthew 5:3

Apprehension and anxiety, yet a calmness possessed me as I reached for the door that led into the church. I asked myself what I was doing here; that I really didn't have anything that I wanted to talk to Rev. Boos about; yet I opened the door and entered. I saw a light on in a room and a voice called out "Hello!"

I walked into a darkish, sparsely furnished office. Along with my other emotions, I now felt bleakly depressed. The room contained one desk, a lamp, bookcase, several pictures and two of the most uncomfortable looking wooden chairs. Rev. Boos smiled and tried to make me feel comfortable. So, we talked about the weather and my dad.

He then asked how he could be of help to me. I told him I didn't know why I was there and that I was feeling confused about something, but didn't know what. We talked about this and somehow got on the subject of gifts.

I didn't understand why some people had gifts that were so different. I found myself talking about my childhood. It seemed as though a dam had broken and much that I had never talked about before came rushing out. I felt high and happy and at ease talking about things that I had kept hidden in my heart and life.

We discussed the subject of extra sensory perception. Why some people know in advance about incidents that are going to happen, when others can't understand them when they are in the middle of such events. Knowing who's phoning before it rings was sometimes a little unnerving, but it is something you get used to; thinking about a person whom you haven't heard from in a long time, then suddenly she or he is there.

I shared with him about my "night visitor" who had come and how much it had frightened me. I told him I thought it had something to do with death and that I was going to die. He said something to me that I had never heard before, that there was more than one kind of death. He said that a person must die spiritually - not physically - before they can really become alive. He suggested that perhaps it had been an angel. In the studies of Scripture in the months that followed, the Lord affirmed this to me. It had indeed been an angel - the announcing angel - it had been Gabriel!!!

We then discussed auras. For me, auras are bands of color that I saw around people. The colors varied as did the width of the bands. I know that some people see these in connection with a person's physical health, but I saw them in connection with their spiritual health, although I didn't understand this until our conversation that night. I thought that <u>everyone</u> saw auras, never mentioning it to anyone. Several other members of my family also see auras around people.

I then told him about the incident which had happened when he came into the Post Office on December 24th - the color, the cape and the dove. He wasn't surprised by anything I said, but had noticed that something had happened to me, he just didn't know what.

We spent several hours talking about people we both knew. He wanted spiritual descriptions and I told him what I saw in them and around them. He wanted to test me further and decided to see if I could tell him about people I had never met but that he knew. We looked though a seminary yearbook and I described accurately every person in it. I even went so far as to inaccurately describe one person - on purpose- and he made me repeat my description. While I was trying to accomplish this, at the same time, I was also thinking to myself, how am I doing this? I don't know these people. I was even more amazed when years later after meeting them, how accurate I had been in my descriptions of them.

This incident was the first time that I knew or felt anything about being held within the power of the Holy Spirit and it was and is like no other power that I know! The Holy Spirit controlled my actions and led me to discern what was happening to me through those following weeks. . . and years.

That evening, we talked like old friends who had known each other for a lifetime and we agreed to talk again. As it turned out, it was sooner than either of us expected.

I returned home that night, feeling as though my heart had suddenly become light, happy, and free. The window to my soul had been opened and the fresh air flowed in freely.

+ A strange Occurrence +

"... "I had a dream,
and my spirit is troubled to know the dream."

Daniel 2:3b

The next morning was Sunday. I suddenly awoke from what I thought had been a bad dream. Tears were rolling down my face. I fell asleep once more and the same dream occurred. Once again I woke up in tears. A third time I slept. Same dream, more tears. I called the church to see if I could talk to Rev. Boos and he answered the phone. He asked me to come to his office.

We met and I related this dream:

It seemed like a large truck was going up the hill into our small town. It had a tan canvas tarp tied to the rear that was flapping in the wind. The pastor was in his car, coming down the hill and when the truck went by the pastor's car vanished."

I didn't understand what it meant, only that for some reason unknown to me, I became frightened and upset. He then said to me, "you can't only see into the future, but also in the past. Last week, I was on my way home and my car brakes failed on that hill; and that truck almost hit me as I was making a left hand turn."

I then told him the only knowledge I had about this dream was that it was a warning to take the car home and not drive it anymore, for it would lead to death.

He agreed to do so. And he did have the money for another car. I then told him exactly what color and model he would buy, for his new car had also been in my dream. And a few days later, I saw him in that exact car.

+ First Instructions +

"Repent therefore,
and turn again,
that your sins may be blotted out,
that times of refreshing may come from
the presence of the Lord,"

Acts 3:19

After Rev. Boos and I talked about the dream, I hesitated and reluctantly told him that a Voice had given me some instructions to carry out. The instructions were to be relayed to him in the sanctuary. Quickly he went with me to the sanctuary.

First I told him that I was afraid. I didn't know what was happening to me or why, but that I had to tell him that I had accepted Jesus Christ in my life as my Savior, Lord, Master and Redeemer. He then asked me if I felt it necessary to confess this to him and was it my first time? I said not really, that several years before I had accepted Him. I told him about the Billy Graham telecast and that nothing had happened to me then. He just smiled and nodded his head very knowingly and affirmatively.

The other instructions I didn't understand, but that we were to go on a journey. We were to go into some type of a house together and then I was to go into the next room alone. I would then be led through that room, out onto a path and then I was to walk the path and go where I was directed by the Holy Spirit.

On our journey, we did find that Jim (he asked me to call him Jim) was to both teach and lead me in interpreting the happenings in and through my life within this extraordinary spiritual experience.

We then prayed together, Jim asking for the wisdom and obedience of Abraham because hadn't Abraham also taken a very long journey? I prayed that any directions I would be given I would follow explicitly. We left the sanctuary and as I moved toward the door, I felt a strong tug in my Spirit, in my heart for I wanted to remain in the warmth and protection of the church walls and the beautiful stained glass windows.

+ First Vision +

*"But Jesus answered, "You do not know what you are asking.
Are you able to drink the cup that I am to drink?"
They said to him, "We are able."*

Matthew 20:22

I stopped in the church again to see Jim on my way home from the Post Office on
New Year's Eve. I felt I needed to relate to him about a strange happening the
night before. I had a picture of Jesus Christ[1] hanging behind the bedroom door,
visible once inside the room. The picture had been a Christmas gift years before.

Once again, I was awakened from a sound sleep, and the picture was not where
I knew it should be. Instead, I saw an image about two feet to the left. The image
was of a Man. The image was illumined and shimmering in the most beautiful
white light. It was the same white color I had seen around THE MAN as a child.

The Man I was seeing was clearly Jesus.
    He was struggling,
        His arms behind Him seemed bound in invisible bonds.
        He was sitting under a swaying palm branch.
          He was trying to free himself;
            His face was turned directly toward me.

There was a silent, yet thunderous, pleading expression on His face. He was
looking directly into my eyes with His tremendous eyes, crying out to me in silence - eyes full of agony - for me to help Him to become free. This pleading lasted
for almost an hour. I ducked my head beneath the blankets thinking He would be
gone when I again looked. But, He was still there!

Finally, my heart began to break, and I cried out, "God, I can't stand to see and
feel any more of His pain." I then tightly closed my eyes.

Waited.   Waited.   Waited.

---

1   Warner Sallman, Portrait of Jesus, 1940

When I finally opened my eyes, Jesus was no longer there. He was gone.

This was my first experience of awareness of the pain of a soul in total tribulation and torment. It is only God who can know my experience of the darkest and deepest agony that I saw in the eyes of Jesus that night, because I cannot explain it any further, this pain I think can ONLY be felt.

+ A New Year, A New Beginning +

"And it shall come to pass afterward,
that I will pour out my Spirit on all flesh;
your sons and your daughters shall prophesy,
your old men shall dream dreams,
and your young men shall see visions."

Joel 2:28

I remember wonderful days with my family but little else between Christmas and New Year's Eve. My emotions seemed in turmoil and yet my very being became excited and I felt deeply challenged. It was the custom of the church to have a Night Watch Service on New Year's Eve. I was most anxious to hear what the sermon subject was for the evening. Jim preached a sermon from Revelation 21:1, "and I saw a new heaven and a new earth."

As I listened to those words, I had no idea what they meant, but I was excited about being in church at the beginning of a New Year. Church was fast becoming for me a comfortable, safe, warm, adventurous place. The turmoil in my emotions became calm and my thoughts were crystal-clear as I spent time in the church building, particularly in the sanctuary. I felt welcomed there. Empty or crowded.

My second vision came this night.

As the service progressed, the words of the Scripture began to burn in my heart and mind. It was then, that I became totally convinced (absolutely convicted) by the Holy Spirit that we are in the last days. And the vision began toward the end of the hour, I looked up toward the ceiling and I saw very clearly on the front wall, on the right corner, an entire city. The city was one built of marble and stone with the design of the buildings as rounded dome roofs and square walled roof tops. There were several spire-topped buildings and they were all of one color - a gleaming, unblemished ivory. I watched as the fire consumed the city, but the buildings were not burning. The red flames grew more and more fierce until they reached the ceiling of the church. The flames extended themselves out through the roof of the sanctuary, and then the vision was gone. I saw this vision for at least 15 minutes. It was a holocaust and to me physical death. I was reminded of the black color I felt at my uncle's funeral. I was also reminded of Moses and his burning bush that did not burn!

I was then given time in years, called the end time. What does this mean?

THE YEARS

2000 to 2002

I pondered on these years often - at the time - and to this very day, I still think of these numbered years. Yes, these years have proved to be devastatingly disastrous for the USA and for our world because of the many, many horrendous, violent events which have taken place.

And the years in-between. . . I understand they will be disastrous years, enduring one calamity, one holocaust after another. The gut feeling I had was that they would NOT be good years. And so far they have not been.

2010 to 2012

Worse is to come. . .

Much, much worse. . .

Horrifically dire. . .

+ Forgotten Memories and Promise, A Conversation +

"I will call to mind the deeds of the Lord;
yea, I will remember thy wonders of old."

Psalm 77:11

In my joy and enthusiasm of my knowledge of a Living God, of His Son, Jesus Christ and the power of the Holy Spirit, came remembrance.

Once again a Voice called to me.   "Darlene"

"Who are you?" I asked. I was totally unprepared for the reply I received.

He said, "Do you remember seeing me when you were a child?
I loved you then as I love you now."

"Yes, I answered. I remember You!
You made me unafraid.
You gave me comfort
You gave me security.
You gave me love."

"Do you remember the promise you made that day in the hospital 19 years ago
- 'If You let him live, You can have me."

"Yes, I remember."

"I have come to collect on that promise. Will you keep your promise?"

"Yes, I will keep my promise."

"I will be with you."

16

+ Joy! Joy! Joy! +

"and you will know the truth,
and the truth will make you free..."

John 8:32

Those first days into the new year were the most satisfying days of my life because they were days filled with God's perfection and His presence. Everyday I triumphantly and joyously glowed, and within my heart and total being there was an overflowing of joy and love as I sang, voiced and even grinned ear to ear as I repeated over and over again...

GOD REALLY IS!
    GOD REALLY EXISTS!
        HEY! GOD IS REAL!
            GOD HAS ALWAYS BEEN!
                GOD WILL ALWAYS BE!
                    GOD IS ALIVE!

GOD GAVE US HIS SON!
    JESUS IS!
        JESUS WAS!

            JESUS ALSO WILL ALWAYS BE!!!

THANK YOU HOLY SPIRIT!

Never in my life do I remember one piece of information affecting me like this knowledge of a living, personal God. . .and to have knowledge of and acceptance of a living personal Savior! Joy! Joy! Joy!

I sang continually, "God is, Jesus is!" in my heart, mind and soul for weeks after this exceptional experience with God and His Son. I woke up singing and fell asleep singing. These were glorious, Son-shining days for at long last, after forty years ~~~

I KNEW HIM! I KNEW THE MAN!!! AND I KNEW THE SON!!!

+ Training Begins +

"And being found in human form
he humbled himself
and became obedient unto death,
even death on the cross."

Philippians 2:8

The first weeks of training in the ways of discipleship kept me in a constant state of deep-seated turmoil in the inner core of my being, with the exception of total peace when I was in the sanctuary of the church.

Obedience was to be the first lesson. It was indeed, the hardest lesson for me to learn. Patience was second! A very far second!

I had been independent in so many ways throughout my life. I could be very headstrong, stubborn and usually, instinctively I knew what to do in most situations. This I believe was an outcome of an abusive mother. Nevertheless, I kept thinking why did I need a Master? I only had myself to rely on...there was no one else, just me I thought. When I undertook a task, I stayed with it until it was finished to my own satisfaction. I looked to perfection in most of my accomplishments and set very high standards as objectives to be reached in all that I did. It was an added aggravation that I felt like I was being "bossed around" even though it was Jesus Christ! And who was THIS Man?

Obedience and the yielding of myself to Christ came slowly and painfully. I found trusting completely, very difficult. It seemed every time I tried to yield, something (or was it somebody?) would turn me the other way - inward, with reliance on myself.

I never knew what was expected of me, or even why. Orders came from and through the Holy Spirit. Orders were:

Do this
            Don't do that
                    Go there
                            Don't go there

And yes, throughout all this training, I kept rebelling. I didn't like orders. It was very difficult at times having such a close relationship/communication access method with the Lord. In this time of training, I became keenly aware of what many of the Old Testament people felt and knew - that conversation with God is not always pleasant or easy. This was a most painful time for me, this time of my disobedience. I wanted to be obedient but was unable. It seemed there was no time for me to reconsider or consider what I was about. When the Lord commands in such a direct method - as Voice - it leaves absolutely no room for disobedience because immediately comes the question, "Why did you do that?" After several "Whys?" I became embarrassed with my disobedience and began to do as I was asked. These lessons in humility lasted for weeks and weeks.

At the very beginning, for instance, I was told to fast for three days. Nothing but water and on the forth day I was to eat, but no meat. I was a diabetic, how would I get through such a fast? And I was to tell no one. I had some anguish throughout those days, yet the Holy Spirit within me was so very powerful that I sailed through my fast. After the fast, I was more alive, more energetic, more clean in mind and more close to the Lord than I would ever have dreamed possible.

Still, the orders came fast, every day and every night. The gifts that I had were now being honed to their limit. Instead of the aura, I now saw color within the eyes of others which allowed me to see the depth of their relationship with the Lord.

White, which was closest to the Lord, I rarely ever saw.
Shades of blue meant varying depths of relationships with the Lord which I frequently saw.
Brown meant a very tentative relationship with the Lord.
Black was rare and meant no relationship with the Lord.

In that period of my conversion I saw every one of the colors. Black was the least of the colors and I only remember seeing black twice.

Slowly, the things that I saw or knew from an earlier time now left me one by one, to be filled with more exciting talents and happenings.

Jim and I began to study Scripture. That is when Jim discovered I knew very little about the Bible. Nevertheless, he scratched his head and suggested we open our Bibles and start to study. He helped me to understand the New Testament through a study of Luke and Acts. At home in the evening, the Holy Spirit taught me wondrous stories from the Old Testament. On my own (?) I read the Psalms for both joy and encouragement.

Sleep. There was one time period at the end of January and the beginning of February that I had a total of eighteen hours of sleep over a three and a half week period. Impossible you say? I have found that nothing is impossible with the Lord! I felt very alive in the Lord and yet felt like a mere robot performing my postal duties to perfection; as a matter of fact, my work was never done better. Studying the Old and New Testaments as I did, was a beautiful, illuminating experience. It was one that I shall never forget, and I still use the knowledge and experience gained during that time, daily.

+ The Gospel Request +

"After this Jesus went out, and saw a tax collector,
named Levi, sitting at the tax office;
and he said to him. "Follow me."
And he left everything, and rose and followed him."

Luke 5:27-28

At our next study time, Jim suggested that we look for answers to our many questions of "Why is this happening?" and "What is the meaning of it all?" In our continuing study of Luke and Acts, we undertook the tedious task of studying the foundation of the church and it was here that Jim quickly found that I was not in even the smallest sense of the word, a Biblical scholar. He found out how very little I actually knew of the history of Christianity and Jesus Christ. As we studied, my thirst for learning became quite intense. For the most part it was a joyous time and as I look back, it was most systematic. From the Old Testament, I began to understand who God is, God's history with people and about their history with God. Especially what I found helpful in this study of God's people, was my study and reading from the Old Testament books of I and II Chronicles.

Through my studies and life's experiences, I came to a stark understanding of the need for EVERY person to accept the Messiah as their personal Savior.

As usual, my home studies were done under the leading and guidance of the Holy Spirit for the Old Testament and the Books of the New Testament. Especially with my studies of James and Peter. As I continued studying with Jim once a week with Luke and Acts, studying Scripture was:

Exciting,
   Challenging,
      Discerning,
         Illuminating,
            Insightful,
               Incisive,
                  Penetrating
                     Piercing
                       Life changing and
Wonderfully different!

From childhood, I had been able to envision vividly in my mind whatever I was reading, yet Scripture came to me as if I were living and seeing the events in reality. Through my mind, emotions and a window in my soul, I saw and was on the site of the area of my studies. I was led by the Holy Spirit as to the appropriate Scripture in my ongoing struggle to grow in my Spirit and build upon my very young faith. During my conversion time, the meaning of Scripture was absolute, clear and certain, and it forced me to grow and develop. I, too, was building my faith upon a solid rock foundation of Jesus Christ, Messiah!

As we studied, we discovered answers to some of my visions and dreams. We began to understand why they had occurred and what they meant. For the most part they had occurred to move me along into a deeper walk into faith and the understanding of discipleship. The more we studied, the more an urgency of unknown meaning began to possess me. I began to feel that I was on an intense time schedule. It felt almost like I was on a speeding train with no hint as to my destination. The only thing that I knew for sure was that my studies of Luke and Acts had to be finished by Easter. I felt locked in and my thought was of death and the color black. Also, that awesome, frightening, black figure that had visited me some two years before came back repeatedly in my thoughts. I asked the Lord if I had been visited by someone He sent and His reply came to me crystal clear, "It was not death but the Angel Gabriel." The pastor put the angel into a category for me: Gabriel was the Announcing Angel. I felt little consolation in that news! After all, he hadn't given me any announcement and there had been no need for scaring me half to death! What did he need to come back and "get me" for? Just what did that mean? No answer came to me.

Nevertheless, the studies began to give me some understanding. One thing that I did understand was that I was very soon to enter into His Kingdom. And it most vividly happened in a dream.

It seemed to be late in the morning and I found myself standing on a broken stone sidewalk, with many other people. There seemed to be no building on either side of the street. We were watching 'something' coming up the cobblestone street. Within the "feeling of electricity" in the air, there seemed to be a quiet, hushed expectation - an expectation that something most unusual was going to happen.

As I looked far down the street, there seemed to be much laughter, jeering and derision aimed at something coming up the street toward us. It looked to me as if some of the crowd were throwing things ~ stones and mud, while others were pointing, spitting and screaming. Yet others were lashing out with sticks and fists. As the 'parade' came nearer to me, the noise became louder and louder. For my first sight, it looked like an elephant moving slowly, tossing its trunk from side to side, but as it came nearer, I could see that it was not an elephant, but a person, bent over dragging something.

As the figure came near enough for me to clearly see , I saw that it was Jesus. He was stumbling and staggering up the street. He was carrying a huge, heavy cross which appeared to be the size of a railroad tie. When He got to where I was standing, He fell down on one knee. It was then that I saw His back. It was raw, the skin was slashed to ribbons, bleeding and dirty. The cross with its rough hewed edges, was digging and cutting into the already exposed flesh. He was sweating, the blood dried in some places and oozing, mingled with the tears of perspiration, in others.

Slowly, very slowly, He turned His face toward me. When this action of His was complete, all became stunningly silent. I could see that His hair was sticky with perspiration, amid the crown of thorns, and I could see the blood trickling from His forehead where a thorn was impaled. Even as He turned His head, it had bumped the cross and the thorns had shifted slightly and I remember vividly thinking and feeling the pain and then crying out to God,

"OH GOD, HOW MUCH THAT MUST HURT HIM!"

His expression caused me to internalize and feel His pain as more intense, more pervading than any pain that I can remember ever happening in my own life.

Jesus' eyes ~ dark blue-green-gray ~ looked into mine, penetrating into every corner of my deepest being. I could hide nothing from those penetrating, haunting, eternal eyes.

He then spoke to me. It did not seem to be a request, command, order or plea. It seemed more like a statement of fact. His voice was gentle, touching and compassionate. He said, "Darlene, do MY will and follow Me."

With those penetrating words I awoke. . .my heart barely beating...my breath loud. . . my mind running at the fastest pace possible. . . The sadness, the pain, the loneliness and the agony that I saw in His eyes seared into my soul, into every fiber of my being. The look in those eyes haunted me. I fought the searing of those eyes with my entire being.

I tried desperately to run from the pain.
> From His eyes.
>> From His voice.
>>> From His firm yet gentle command to me.

I complained!
I grumbled!
I growled!

Everyone around me felt my unhappiness, Jim, my family, and the Lord. I laid myself at the throne of God. Just how dare He DO this to Me? And anyway, what sane person in this 20th Century has things like this experience happen? I tried running but no matter what I did or tried, those haunting eternal eyes were there, searching mine. . . waiting. Patiently waiting. Every time that I blinked, I looked into His eyes.

I stood up against the pressure of His eyes for about two weeks and finally, gratefully, I yielded. Jim and I were studying one evening, and I felt called into the sanctuary. I don't know how to express this happening other than I felt Jesus knocking at my being. I went into the sanctuary, felt I could stand no more and went down on my knees. I then asked Him to come into my life, forgive me of my sins and to do with me as He willed. It was then that "I KNEW HIM: I knew Him as my personal Savior." Accepting the Savior made me free!

FREE!

But then, how can one be bound to following and be free at the same time? Yet, I did know the kind of joy that occurs with such an experience. I found being free in the soul gave me the ability for unlimited soaring of my Spirit. What a great, loving experience, what a gift! It compares with nothing that I can think of except perhaps, death. The soul has the capability to soar throughout the universe and be on earth at one and the same time. The soaring allows for the acquiring of knowledge to happen instantaneously. Before such an experience though, the whole idea of such a happening is unthinkable. BUT, what an experience! God allowed me to work through many things, such as my stubbornness, being impatient, feeling unworthy, being unsure, working through my experiences of abuse, etc. which allowed me to come to my own decision and my intense desire to follow Jesus Christ. I have never regretted the time spent in knowing myself and have been grateful to God, Jesus and the Holy Spirit for the patience given to me in those weeks which gave me such freedom from self, yet for self!

Jesus then said, "Prepare for baptism." My tears came, flushing out the sins of my life, the rejections and abuse in my life, while being replaced with/by ~ at the same time ~ baptism through the Holy Spirit. I was not frightened and I remember the feeling of peaceful contentment that came over me even before it began. The baptism began as a consuming fire, starting with my mind and going through my entire body. I was in a conversation with the Lord the whole time this was happening. It seemed to start out as a red hot fire but was completely white as it "cleansed" me. The white was like the white glow that I had seen around God anytime that I looked at Him, beginning when I saw Him as THE MAN as a three year old child.

When the baptism was completed, I felt clean, pure and innocent ~ beautifully and wonderfully free. And when in my mind's eye I looked at Jesus, His magnificent white robe was now a light blue, the color change I took to be the stains of my sins, because He had unconditionally accepted me, and had graced me with a new birth, a new life, and a new beginning.

The fire of this cleansing did not leave me completely, as part of it seemed to stay within my heart and much of the time, even today, I can feel its heat, its warmth. This fire is now as much a part of my life as breathing. This first cleansing happened on a Wednesday night.

The second cleansing happened on a Saturday afternoon, some two weeks later. This one also came as Jim and I were studying Scripture. For whatever reason, Jim and I began to talk about my traumatic childhood and then my later years. As I was talking to Jim about my traumatic childhood and later years, Jim said to me, "Do you see the water flowing in from the corner of the room, past my elbow into you?" I said, "I couldn't see it but was sure feeling it." I felt lighter and lighter as we talked. The circumstances of my life which I talked about had also never been shared with anyone else before this day.

The third cleansing came after another two weeks and also came on a Saturday. It was the most difficult for me to get through. It began as a white light and seemed to be illumining. It also began spiraling down through the top of my head and went down into and through my entire body. But this time there was some pain. As it entered me, the white turned into a red fire and felt more like a searing, burning sensation than anything else. This cleansing left its mark on me and it hurt so much that I cried. Jesus was once again talking to me, comforting me. He was talking to me about the pain that He had felt and I too, now had knowledge of a tiny portion of His pain. It is still with me ~ both the knowledge and the pain.

Why these three happenings? I know that my life was in need of such a cleansing but I do not know the 'whys' for certain. I just know that they did occur and for such experiences, I thank the Lord because the Lord knew what my needs in the future would be and these three experiences turned into ones of comfort for me. I have never known such love as He was with me within those cleansings. The tenderness and knowledge of the Lord comforting me from age three, is a tenderness and a Presence that I try to share with others day by day.

Some time within these three happenings I was healed of diabetes. I was checked by three different physicians and I received the same verdict from each of them, no diabetes.

19

+ Abstinence from Food, Feeds the Soul +

"And when you fast, do not look dismal. . ."

Matthew 6:16a

Two fasts occurred within this four month period. The first came early in my experience which I have already described. Nothing by mouth for three days and no meat on the fourth day. I knew nothing about fasting, and I did as the Lord asked. I agreed to fast if the Lord would do 'something' about stomach noises. There were none. At the end of the third day, I felt exhilarated and I felt as though I were in perfect unity with everything around me, particularly with the Lord. To Him I seemed especially attuned and in perfected oneness.

The second fast came during Holy Week. My instruction was to take nothing except water after The Lord's Supper on Maundy Thursday until my family and I became members of the Memorial Presbyterian Church on Easter morning.

Yes, when fasting, hunger is very present but for each hunger pang there are compensations. Fasting is something that I will continue to do for several reasons. Two such good reasons are wanting to be as spiritually attuned to the Trinity as possible and the knowing that hunger makes you depend entirely upon the Lord for ALL your needs, both spiritual and physical. The other reason is that I will to do it because fasting is one thing that I can make up my mind to do to demonstrate to the Lord that I care about Him in a physical way as well as in a spiritual way.

Fasting gives an utter sense of oneness between the physical body and the spiritual body. It allows integration of both 'bodies' acknowledging what it is that makes me ~ me, and you ~ you. Fasting allows a peaceful interaction between the systems and the integrating of their function within. Inside this unity which occurs, I find that all my being is disciplined to a total dependence upon the Lord, and that life is wholly meaningful. The two gifts, peace and perfection in union with the Lord, is only part of the experience. This interaction between the body and soul allows for hunger to disappear.

Also, in this union with the Lord, knowledge is pure and alive. Who is it that gives the peace that passes all understanding that is so talked about? Who is the bread of life? The answer to both questions is Jesus Christ. Jesus, for me is the joy of fasting. Never to hunger or thirst again. Yes, the flesh of the body does hunger and thirst, but the soul, even the mind and the emotions understand fully, the answer to the question, "Why was I born, why am I here?" The hunger and thirst in these questions is answered for all time for each individual. I know that I am here only to honor, glorify and love the Lord with everything that I am, do and have in my life.

Fasting also gives a sense of unity between your total being and the Holy Trinity. It causes the senses within the body and soul to become pure and to have your entire being channeled into thought and expression of adoration to God. This world of holiness is unique and awesome.

Just for four days. It is enough to allow entrance into the Presence of the Lord. If fasting is done in humility and prayer, the heart becomes deeply touched and moved, and through this activity the body and soul are cleansed, inside and out, in both reality and in actuality. Communion with God through Jesus Christ, by the Holy Spirit is the fruit of fasting. Answers come. Peace comes. This peace is the food that this world needs to dine on. . . daily, hourly and perhaps even each and every second!

+ Ministry +

"Go therefore and make disciples of all nations,
baptizing them in the name of the Father
and of the Son and of the Holy Spirit,"

Matthew 28:19

As early as January 14, 1974, I knew that the Lord was calling me into ministry but didn't know what kind. Jim and I were standing talking in the church doorway one evening. He stopped talking, hesitated, looked at me and said, "The Lord is calling you into ministry..." and my reply was, "I was just going to tell you the Lord is calling me into ministry..." We smiled broadly at each other. The idea of ministry had been placed in both our minds at the exact moment, NOT an unusual happening to us in those months. It is my belief that this particular pastor was quite attuned to the impulses of the Holy Spirit and without his belief in the utter leading of the Lord in his life, we would have never met, nor would I have been able to have had such a conversion experience. I took vast amounts of his time, which was an embarrassment to me, for I knew how busy his ministry was each and every day. Yet, when I would apologize, he would tell me it was a learning experience for him too.

Indeed, I would not have known the Lord or the meaning of salvation, except that a stranger who was not ashamed of the Gospel, the Rev. Dr. James Boos of the Memorial Presbyterian Church, came my way.

+ Out of Sight +

"Hear my cry, O God,
listen to my prayer;
from the end of the earth I call to thee,
when my heart is faint.
Lead thou me
to the rock that is higher than I;
for thou art my refuge,
a strong tower against the enemy.
Let me dwell in thy tent for ever!
Oh to be safe under the shelter of thy wings!"

Psalm 61:1-4

I began to have some anxiety about Easter week toward the end of January. The Lord told me that it would be some kind of a trial and the only thing that I knew for sure was that I could see nothing beyond Black Friday. I did know that death would be certain for me because it came clearly to me that I would walk the path that Jesus had walked during His final week. I knew that I was clearly to walk in the valley of the shadow of death and I was definitely not to be afraid! King David's utterly wonderful, meaningful words and thoughts found in Psalm 23.

The color black gave me an intense, deep fear as it walked me back through all the black happenings of my life to understand and grow because of them.

Nevertheless, I was still on my exciting pilgrimage. I was now out on the path from the rooms that Jim and I had entered. I was alone and as I was walking up a slight grade of a well trod path, I found myself looking up at the image of God, THE MAN that I had seen as a child. This time, Jesus was standing halfway up the stairway between God and me. I stood at the bottom of the stairs, seeing them both with the blue sky and white clouds behind them.

Suddenly, I knew that I would see God no more and I was taken by the Holy Spirit and whisked high upon a mountain top. When I looked at the Throne Room, there came a white cloud between my vision and where God was standing. I was then enclosed in a four sided, brown canvas tent.

I was led to read Psalm 27 and it sustained me. Actually I felt that it had been written just for me! The words gave me both courage and strength.

Verse 5, particularly comforted me.

"For He will hide me in the shelter in the day of trouble;
He will conceal me under the cover of his tent,
He will set me high upon a rock"

These words were of great meaning to me and for me.

I didn't like being so shut in and so I asked Jim to intercede for me. He did, offering one of his beautiful prayers on my behalf, and the Lord opened one tent wall and I could then see the blue sky and the clouds before the throne of God.

Even with one wall opened for me, I still felt shut in, and I began to maintain the strictest of attention to God and God's will for me. I began to study the Old Testament in a depth that I had not been able to accomplish before this latest event. Here in the seclusion of a 'tent', began my affection for the stories, meanings and characters of the Old Testament. These people of old who followed God's will for their lives have my utmost admiration for I came to know through their lives that mine was no easier nor harder than any of theirs, except that I have the great advantage of having Jesus Christ in my life. Indeed, I did discover that people have not advanced one iota since the dawn of humankind's history on this earth. Our personalities have not been able to eliminate greed, power, selfishness, lust, brutality, war or the many other things that are ugly in our world. In my studying about, and meeting of those Old Testament people, I have found hope but even more than that, I have found that God's love of us is steadfast! And eternal.

+ A Beautiful Interlude +

"Therefore the Lord himself will give you a sign.
Behold, a young woman shall conceive and bear a son,
and shall call his name Immanuel."

Isaiah 7:14

Another vision happened on January 28th. I saw a star, shining brilliantly in a darkened sky. I was told to go to it. As I lay there trying to reach up to it, I felt my Spirit leave my body trying to reach it. It was one of the strangest sensations that I have ever felt. The 'alive' part of me was looking down at my body in bed, yet my body was alive for I could see it breathing. Once again, I became frightened. What was happening? This seemed so unreal. I said to the Lord that I was frightened and Jesus told me to return to my body and I did. Before I had become so frightened, I had gotten about halfway to the star, and I remembered what I had been able to observe. I could see a large part of the earth and it was breathtakingly, utterly beautiful. I could see some faces and a large area of land. There were shepherds, the City of Bethlehem with many people milling around and the star with its illuminating light. I saw the outside of an inn and a few camels. It was starkly, serenely peaceful and still. I have never known the quietness of such a scene. It was night yet the starlight made it as day. Too beautiful to describe actually!

When I had become so frightened the vision stopped. It did continue later in a dream but it was vastly different.

In this dream, the star was shining just as brilliantly but this time very slowly, the manger descended down a shaft of light that was shining from the star. The manger came almost within touching distance. By some method unknown to me, I went halfway up the shaft of light to meet it. We met just out of my touching it for when I saw the Baby, I reached out and my arms and heart ached because I could neither touch nor hold Him. The manger was bathed in a brilliant white light, more pure than the flowing light from the star. Then just as slowly, the manger ascended back up the shaft of light toward the star. I realized that my eyes had been gifted with seeing perfection coming to earth, lying in a manger.

+ Ultimate Love +

"Because thy steadfast love is better than life,
my lips will praise thee."

Psalm 63:3

Psychological happenings! For me the visions, dreams and pressures I felt from the Holy Spirit; criticisms from some and support from others, condemnation from others and being dependent on Jim for understanding. Who would believe any of this – who could or would - except me and Jim?

I began to think that perhaps I was insane or slowly going insane. For about a half an hour I considered suicide. I felt that no one understood for certain just what was happening to me. And who really cared? A pastor who had known me for a very short time? Never. I said to myself that I would be better off dead. Anyhow, what about suicide? What is life actually worth to anyone else? Who hears such voices? Only 'crazy' people. Death would have to be better than this kind of insanity. I was surely going insane I thought. I didn't want to live with this kind of pain or crazy experience.

I had met with Jim that evening and never told him about my thoughts of suicide. I sat in my car after our Scripture lesson and the tears flowed. I thought that Jim had left the parking lot and through my tears and questions to myself, I heard the crunch of gravel beside my car. I looked up and saw him standing beside my window. He asked if I was OK. I assured him that I really was fine and he left.

I started my car and went slowly down the hill of the road that led out of town and said to myself, "Why not?" It would be quick and easy.

With that quick thought, the Lord's voice came to me. "Darlene, I WILL hold you in the palm of My hand in death, but that is not the plan I have set for you." I quickly thought about His offer to accept me, even as a suicide, and of all the other experiences which He had shared with me, all the gifts that had already been given to me. How many people on this earth have ever actually seen Jesus? His eyes came to me and I realized how VERY ridiculous were my thoughts of suicide. I had my Savior and salvation, what did I care what others thought of me ~ or said to me to support me or otherwise ~ or what they thought of my wondrous experience? I absolutely knew. . .what was true for me.

Did this fear arise from my abused background? I presumed so.

Scripture was always there when I needed it. The Holy Spirit led me to open my Bible and read Psalm 27.

> Absolutely I knew. . .
>> The Lord is MY light!
>>> The Lord is MY salvation!
>>> The Lord is MY Savior!

Why then should I be fearful or intimidated?

The next day, I talked with Jim about my thoughts of suicide, of my mental, psychological, emotional condition and the circumstances of my experiences. Together we decided that I needed a health checkup. I first talked with my own physician who never spends time on useless advice. When he gives his opinion, he expects and anticipates that you will follow his advice. As he was examining me, I told him what had been happening to me. He looked at me and said, "Darlene, listen to the voice and do what is asked. If you don't, you will regret it the rest of your life." He found no physical or mental problems with me.

The second physician also had no problems with occurring dreams and visions. He said, "just because God didn't work that way with many people, there was no reason that He couldn't work that way with me if He so chose." This particular physician knew in advance about my experiences almost from the beginning, as Jim and I had agreed that he was to share any of my experience with the session of the church and this doctor, who was a most beloved member of the church and community.

The third physician was a stranger to me, recommended to me by my brother, Alfie and was his doctor. I told him about my visions and dreams as he was examining me. I was sitting on the examining table and he opposite me. In the middle of our conversation, he reached over and slightly touching my arm, said, "God bless you. There's nothing wrong with you. Go and do as you are being told. . . and let me know how you progress." This physician was no longer a stranger, but a dear and caring friend.

With such words, the doubts that had crept into my mind were erased. I continued my journey a little more confident in people that I had previously felt or experienced.

24

+ Ecstasy +

*"In that day you will know that I am in my Father,
and you in me, and I in you."*

John 14:20

Ecstasy is a word that most people do not understand. Those who read the Spiritual Masters or mystics, such as St. John of the Cross or Ste Teresa of Avila know the meaning of the word. Some people say, "But they were Catholic Saints weren't they?" Others comment that "things like that do not happen in the Protestant traditions."

I only know that it happened to me supremely, once.

I encountered a most perfect day. Spring was in the air and the sun was shining, the earth warming. I was in harmony with nature and content with everyone and with all that was happening in my life.

I had stopped at the church office to speak with Jim for a moment, but he was on the telephone. I went into the sanctuary and my heart began to overflow with love for God and Jesus. I thought of all the wondrous things that God had done for Creation and yes, even for me! I went to my knees in prayer and praise. I felt as though I was in the Throne Room once again, at the feet of THE MAN and all that I could feel was overwhelming love. I remember raising my arms toward Him, then reaching out to touch Him. Slowly, as I came nearer to Him, we seemed to touch and it was then that I became one with God, Jesus, the Holy Spirit and the universe. Within the same moment, I had now ~ somehow ~ became surrounded by and penetrated with the purity of that illumining, shimmering white light. It was perfection. It was clean and pure. In this touching of love, all fears of death and life were gone. I was in this state for at least thirty minutes, (as Jim later told me, as he had heard the door scrape open and close when I entered the sanctuary) although it seemed like seconds to me. As I came to myself in the sanctuary, I felt my knees touch down upon the carpet of the step. Somehow, I had now experienced levitation. And perfection.

The experience of such a oneness with God and the Son, through the power of the Holy Spirit, is the ultimate event which can happen in any human life. We cannot seek it out nor can we demand such an occurrence. It does not come for the wants or needs of any individual. Why anyone is graced with such an experience is only known by God. It is God alone who initiates such oneness.

Once so touched, the event is never forgotten because the knowledge and warmth of it is always intermingled in the mind, being and Spirit.

25

+ Farewell My Friend +

"And God said, "This is the sign of the covenant
which I make between me and you
and every living creature that is with you,
for all future generations:
I set my bow in the cloud,
and it shall be a sign of the covenant
between me and the earth."

Genesis 9:12-13

I was invited by the youth fellowship of the church to their winter retreat. It was held in a mountainous area of northwestern Pennsylvania. It was a beautiful camp and it was a good day for driving. It was very cold, but the sun was shining. It was one of those winter days when it is great just being alive and out of doors. I had just gotten out of the car when I heard the Lord speak. He gave me instructions to be followed immediately. I had never been there before, yet I started to walk the path He told me to take and before long I was running. I ran down a hill and through the woods and came upon an empty cabin, located beside a small stream. The stream was crystallized, beautifully frozen along its banks with the water in the center babbling along at a hurried pace. On the banks of this stream I was told to sit down. It was damp and misty, but I found a comparatively dry rock and sat comfortably down.

I looked up and across the stream, beholding an image of the Face of God. It was the closest, most clear image I was ever to see. God's face was three dimensional, and all but touched mine, or did it? It was not a full view but slightly turned to the right. It was THE MAN that I remembered. It was that same loving face that had helped me to continue my life from the age of three. It seemed to be about twenty feet in length and perhaps ten feet in width. God never looked at me directly, but told me gently and quietly, "Be still and listen." I heard these words, "It is time for us to say farewell. We will never see each other again like this on earth." I was then shown a panorama of my life, past - present - future.

Once again the Lord had chosen a unique way of telling me what was wanted of me and why I was being called. This panorama vision happened very quickly. It was like a slide show that is on the screen for a couple of seconds before moving onto the next picture.

God, then said, "Farewell, my friend." The image then began to slowly fade into the mist of the hillside and the tugging already in my being of loneliness, so quick to happen, made me feel gently sad. Not ever to see my Friend again. Tears came and were cold as they streamed down my cheeks. A verse of Scripture crossed through my mind.

"Blessed are they who have not seen and yet believe." John 20:29.

I sat quietly watching the babbling stream through my tears, and then wiped my tears and looked up. In the exact spot where the image of the Face had been, I saw distinctly and clearly a beautiful, brilliant, complete rainbow. The sadness in my heart and soul became joy and they began to sing.

I sat for some time in awe, mixed with a feeling of peace, contentment and love, just one with the message and quiet.

On my way home, I thought deeply about the events of the day and I knew this event would forever be firmly locked within my heart and mind's eye. Even today, it is revived each time I see a rainbow. It had been a quiet, touching yet powerful experience.

26

+ School? At my age? +

"Keep hold of instruction, do not let her go;
guard her, for she is your life."

Proverbs 4:13

Jim was leading the youth retreat, had invited me to join them for an afternoon of discussion about avocations, and when I finally joined them, he knew
that something joyous had happened to me, but time prevented us from discuss-
ing it for several days. When we did talk about it, we discussed both the sadness
and the joy of such an experience. He assured me, probably for the 100th time,
that God's leading my life in such a way would cause a new experience to begin
for me.

The first happening came as a new voice, that of the Holy Spirit speaking to
me. I was to begin to tithe, ten percent of the gross of my salary. I did.

My studies continued in the unusual, unique way as before. In conjunction
with Luke and Acts, I had begun an unusual journey with Abraham. While
I was reading the Old Testament, I began to see, hear and feel the story of
Abraham more than I actually read or studied it. I did not like Abram at the beginning, a matter of fact I was furious with him for lying to protect himself. On
top of that, he gave away his wife! How could someone who had such a great
relationship with God do that? As I understand the growth and development
of Abraham, I began to understand faith and felt my own faith developing. As I
was studying, I saw a vision, it was the downward swing of the arm of Abraham
with the knife to sacrifice his son and then I heard the voice say "STOP!" I re-
flected later long and hard about this action, and with a sudden clarity, I understood it. All comes from God, does not God have the right to request anything
and everything of us? All includes the giving of our children which can be many
ways!

After Abraham I began to study on Moses. I learned from him about the Ten
Commandments. It was a living experience. This learning took one month to
complete.

"The Ten Commandments." A very private, personal matter these Ten
Commandments. Tough laws indeed!

The Ten Commandments

Commandment One

"And <u>Jesus</u> said to him,
"You shall love the Lord your God with all your heart,
and with all your soul, and with all your mind.
This is the great and first commandment."

Matthew 22:37-38

My duty to God.   First in my heart and life.   First in my heart.

How could I not love the Lord with all my being? He loved me and set me free. Yet, it was freedom within obedience. I felt like I had arrived at a lake and had been afraid to dive in, afraid of sinking and drowning. Yet, when I did jump in I felt no fears at all. I found the more I swam, the more room there was to be obedient, and how much larger the lake became, actually endless. I was afraid of restriction, yet found in obedience, a joy in the ability given to me to make my own decision in choices. My choices were made much easier by my being aware of what truth is as I encountered truth in the whole of the Jesus event through my experiencing of Him.

The Lord my God is first in my life and I try to live the truth of the Gospel. Finding truth is not an easy discipline. I am still working on this one - and will probably never get it completely accomplished, for it is exceedingly difficult.

Commandment Two

"You shall have no other gods before me."

Exodus 20:3

This commandment means that God is first and foremost in our entire life and being. First in our thoughts, our feelings, our actions, and our motivations.

Commandment Three

"You shall not take the name of the Lord your God in vain;
for the Lord will not hold him guiltless who takes his name in vain."

Exodus 20:7

You shall not take the name of the Lord your God in vain...swearing. This is just something that I rarely ever do. I was told long ago by one of my teachers that if you have a good command of the English language, there should never be a need for any swear words. I took her at her word!

Commandment Four

"Remember the sabbath day, to keep it holy."

Exodus 20:8

Remember to keep the Sabbath Day Holy. I began to see each day as a Holy Day not just Sunday. I learned to rest in the Lord daily and have, to the best of my abilities, not allowed myself to become a Sunday – one-day-a-week Christian.

Commandment Five

"Honor your father and your mother,
that your days may be long in the land
which the Lord your God gives you."

Exodus 20:12

Honoring my parents was difficult. It took me years but it was accomplished through the act of forgiveness, done within myself realizing that Christ had already forgiven me for my sins. I knew from my study of what it should be, but the act of honor came when I fully realized that the death and resurrection of Jesus, freely gave me worth! The feeling of worth that I experienced gave to me a security which no one has ever been able to even slightly scratch, not in the slightest. It is an anchor which I will never lose. He had reached out His hand to me, He forgave me. Could I do less for my parents: when I forgave, I saw their worth too. Had they not brought me and my siblings into this world healthy children? Very healthy!

Commandment Six

"You shall not kill."

Exodus 20:13

Killing. It has been my nature to abhor violence. To me murder is insanity. Another person. An unborn child. It surges in me again the question, "What is the worth of a person?" Murder is crucifying Christ all over again and when that occurs, it only causes more pain and agony. And guilt. Huge guilt.

Commandment Seven

"You shall not commit adultery."

Exodus 20:14

Adultery is always wrong. It destroys minds, emotions, relationships and lives. It destroys self worth.

Commandment Eight

"You shall not steal."

Exodus 20:15

Stealing. I recall a first hand story of this in my life. It is an embarrassment for me, nevertheless, when I was about 9, I stole a bottle of fingernail polish (I didn't even wear polish) and almost got caught. When the clerk approached me, I dropped it down into my umbrella. She asked me to show her my hands, I did, but of course they were empty. Almost got caught. Later, I walked back to her section in the store and replaced it in the bin. Fear has its goodness. It scared me to think about the reaction from my mother.
I never stole another item.

Commandment Nine

"You shall not bear false witness against your neighbor."

Exodus 20:16

Lying is something that I thought I never did but came face to face with it also. I had received a telephone call from someone I didn't want to talk with. What a response! "Mother, isn't that lying?" Embarrassed, I did talk to the person and never asked my children to do that for me again!

Commandment Ten

You shall not covet your neighbor's house;
you shall not covet your neighbor's wife,
or his manservant, or his maidservant,
or his ox, or his ass,
or anything that is your neighbor's."

Exodus 20:17

You shall not covet. Coveting was for me the easiest law not to break because I never cared much for, or about, material things. You can only live in one place at a time, drive one vehicle at a time and wear one piece of clothing at a time. This in fact turned out to be a positive law for me because I see in it the opportunity to share. It made tithing easy. It is great to feed the hungry or 'fix-up' a room or build a house! Habitat for Humanity, Heifer Project, Salvation Army and giving my blood, are four of my favorite opportunities. To help others anyway possible is what we Christian's are called to do. The feeling one gets from helping others is a great bonus to being a Christian!

Jesus reaffirms six of these Commandments in Mark 10:19.

"You know the commandments:
    'Do not kill,
        Do not commit adultery,
            Do not steal,
                Do not bear false witness,
                    Do not defraud,
                        Honor your father and mother'."

The Commandment lessons were an especially emotional time for me, yet I have remembered each lesson well. I have disciplined myself in trying to obey them in all the situations occurring in my life. Not easy. The passing years have caused what were once 'simple' commandments to become complex and now takes more thinking and meditating time in arriving at decisions of the truth.

During this time of learning about the Commandments, I had another vision.

I was looking into a sunrise. I could see someone coming out of the wilderness. I waited as he came near and from the way that he was dressed, I knew it to be John the Baptist. Suddenly, he disappeared and a small boy appeared and continued to walk toward me. As he walked he changed several times before becoming a young man. It seemed to be Christ, but as he came close to me, he changed, with his heart now on the outside of his chest. It was extremely hot and dry in this wilderness and the sunrise caused much glare. It made it very difficult for me to see. As the young man came close to me, he offered me his hand and I clasped his hand and looked into his face and then into his eyes. Suddenly the handsome, young face, turned into an ugly, grotesque face. And he was laughing.

As I looked into his eyes, the deeper I looked, the more I saw my own temptations. My own salvation then came to me by words that I spoke to him. I quoted the words of Jesus, "It is written, you shall worship the Lord your God, and him only shall you serve"... this the beginning of Jesus' temptation story found in Luke 4.

Once again, Psalm 27:1 came to me, and then just as suddenly, I found myself walking again in the hot, dry, beautiful wilderness. This time though, I was walking with Christ holding onto my hand and I felt that I was about 5 years old. We walked through the wilderness and then by the Sea of Galilee. As we walked, we felt the stillness of the air and heard the sea as it gently lapped upon the shore. As we walked onto the pier, I heard Jesus call to some men who were working on their fishing nets. He said to them, "Come Peter, Come Andrew, Come James, Come John." They were simply said words yet seemed vibrant commands. There was something about the quality of that Voice...

We then walked further and came to a house. As we approached the doorway, Jesus lifted me onto a wooden crate which allowed me to look into a room through an open window. He entered the house, spoke to people in the room and sat down. As they continued talking, I noticed movement in the ceiling. A hole was made and a cot was lowered into the room. I saw the miraculous healing of the paralytic and participated in the joy of all the people in the room because of this miracle.

I felt that I never left that window area, yet at the same time, I was still holding onto his hand for more journeying.

Jim and I discussed this vision but didn't discover its meaning for me.

We also discussed some further voice instructions that I had received. The instructions were for me to attend the University of Pittsburgh and the Pittsburgh Theological Seminary. I was to complete my education in six years. Further, I was not to do anything about entrance into the university until after Easter. Moreover, I was to resign my position with the post office because I could no longer work for both God and mammon. My last day of work was to be Good Friday.

Oh! Oh! The University of Pittsburgh! An answer to a long ago secret heart's desire. I remembered, that after high school I had wanted to go to college but there was no money for me to attend the university. I was to go back to school at the age of 40??? Oh! Why hadn't the Lord called me at age 30? or 20?

This decision of mine caused many reactions in our small community.

- "You are just going too far!
- Just who is going to feed your kids, they will starve, after all you should think of them first!
- God doesn't call women.
- You are going through the change of life.
- Can I have your job?
- You can't quit!
- You will never make it through college at your age!
- You are the Antichrist.
- I think you have gone overboard."

These among many other negative statements and emotions of envy, jealousy, anger and hatred directed at me.

But there were many other kinds of reactions also:

- "It's wonderful!
- You will do very well in that profession.
- I can't think of anyone else that could do better in ministry than you!
- I think that it is marvelous that you are being called.
- Whatever you want to do is okay.
- Do what is best for you.
- I am really happy for you.
- God bless you."

I did take people seriously because I knew that most of them did genuinely care about me and my family. But, I decided that my first priority was to God and believed in God's will for my life. After all, no one else cared enough about me to pay the cost that His Son was sent to pay for my salvation.

Actually, changing my life in the middle of the stream was easier than I ever dreamed possible. Excitement and challenge had been part of my life since I had been a child and not knowing what was to become of me was certainly an exciting tug at my life. I have never regretted my decision and I have not looked back, wanting to keep my face pointed toward the future and reunion one day with God and Jesus.

27

+ Another Conversation +

"When they had finished breakfast,
Jesus said to Simon Peter,
"Simon, son of John, do you love me more than these?"
He said to him, "Yes Lord; you know that I love you."
He said to him, "Feed my lambs."
A second time he said to him, "Simon, son of John, do you love me?"
He said to him, "Yes Lord; you know that I love you."
He said to him, "Tend my sheep."
He said to him the third time, "Simon, son of John, do you love me?"
Peter was grieved because he said to him a third time, "Do you love me?"
And he said to him, "Lord, you know everything; you know that I love you."
Jesus said to him. "Feed my sheep."

John 21:15-17

One of the three physicians that I had an appointment with for my last physical checkup lived in Virginia. During this trip, I heard the voice of Jesus say in a soft, even tone...

"Darlene, do you love me?"	"Yes, Lord, you know that I do!"
"Darlene, do you really love me?"	"Yes, Lord, you know that I do!!"
"Darlene, do you love me?"	"Yes, Lord, you know that I do!!!"

The first question I answered in sincere honesty for I was startled at both the voice and the questions. The second question was answered with almost the same tone as the first, but I asked myself, "Why is He asking when He already knows the answer?" The third time I answered with some force. "Lord what a ridiculous question. You know . . ."

And then I laughed to myself for I heard the laughter of Peter in my mind as I remembered his answers to the same questions. When they had finished breakfast, "Jesus said to Simon Peter, "Simon, son of John, do you love me more than these?" He said to him, "Yes, Lord; you know that I love you." He said to him, "Feed my lambs." A second time he said to him, "Simon, son of John, do you love me?" He said t him, "Yes Lord; you know that I love you." He said to him, "Tend my sheep." he said to him the third time, "Simon, son of John, do you love me?" and he said to him, "Lord you know everything; you know that I love you." Jesus said to him, "Feed my sheep." And after this he said to him, "Follow me." This scripture comes from John 21:15-17b. From this I note that we humans surely are an impatient lot. And I said to myself but aloud, "Oh Lord, will I ever learn?"

28

+ A Very Long Week. . . +

"A little while, and you will see me no more;
again a little while, and you will see me."

John 16:16

All through my journey these past months, the thought was always in the back of my mind, that horrid black color in which I could neither see or feel anything. In my mind it recalled to me the pain of rejection as a child when I was in that "blackened" living room. And too, I seemed unable to forget the words of Gabriel, who had also come in the black of the night, as did my deep remembrances of abuse, saying, I'll be back for you." Formerly, I'd no understanding of death, just that once dead everything was over, just black remained. There was no 'beyond'. There was nothing. And wasn't that just what I had seen at my uncle's funeral? There wasn't anything beyond the grave. However, in the past months, death took on new meaning and I had come to have no fear of it. A physical death meant little for I knew where I would be spending eternity and I rather look forward to it. But, the anxiety of the notion of the black color and its unknown depth was always in the forefront of my thinking, consciously and unconsciously. In my thinking, the color black still meant to me, rejection, cold rejection.

As early as January, I had known that a trial would be coming to test my faith. Would it endure? Would I endure? Throughout all the months of my conversion experience, I knew of nothing which was to happen to me beyond Good Friday. I had already been told by voice instruction, that I would be walking the path that Christ walked in His final week. What would happen to me on Saturday? I only knew that some of my fear about Holy Week had to do with the visions I'd had at the very beginning. That very first time, when I saw the shimmering image of Jesus on my wall, the agony in His eyes had become part of my soul and had been reinforced by the several other times that our eyes had met. In walking the valley of the shadow of death, could I be free of fear?

After all my experiences and all the teachings of the Lord, the Holy Spirit and from Jim, would my faith be strong enough to see me through more pain or perhaps a new intense experience? I was new in the way of Christianity, new in the Lord. My conversion had been intense in both time and training. And so, in prayer and meditation, I sat down and retraced those past fleeting months, in both my mind and emotions. I'd had both joy and pain in the training for the Lord's call.

He was so very exacting with me and I rebelled time after time not hurting anyone but myself and perhaps the Lord. There came pain after pain, pain in knowing the world's sins and my own, yet these pains were mingled with many joys that gave to me a type of sanity.

Each time that I would disobey, the Lord would shut doors and close me in, to teach me many invaluable lessons;

Know yourself,
Know your strengths,
Know your weaknesses and yes,
Know why you behave as you do.
But most of all, like yourself!

Especially, did He say to me, "Darlene, like yourself because it is I who give to your life worth and value. Your life is worth my death. I died for you, be of that worth!"

I try daily to be of that worth, and only hear Paul's words in Romans 7:15 ringing in my ears, "I do not understand my own actions. For I do not do what I want, but I do the very thing I hate..." BUT, I, like Paul, keep trying and this part of my life is different from the past because the love of the Lord is there to sustain me and give me the strength to keep going forward. Trusting was very hard for me, for I thought that my whole life was dependent upon only one person- ME! Who needed me? Yes, my family needed me in their lives, but I found that Jesus needed me ~ Christ needed me as His disciple and I needed Him because each time that I stumbled, he was there to help me understand my problems and to set me back on my life's journey.

Once again, as they frequently did, my thoughts returned to my uncle's funeral and the memory of that service. I remembered once again my emotions being drained away and only being able to see black. I was in so much despair that I thought my heart would break in his remembrance.

I tried in my thoughts to see through the eyes and emotions of Jesus about death. More understanding came as I pondered about the meaning of death.

I now found myself in the last week. At the very least, I would now have the final answers about life, faith and death ~ very swiftly!

29

+ Palm Sunday +

*"So they took branches of palm trees
and went out to meet him, crying,
'Hosanna!
Blessed is he who comes in the name of the Lord,
even the King of Israel!"*

John 12:13

The dream sequence of my walking along with Jesus, once again continued. I was now no longer looking in the window, but found myself standing once again on the sidewalk. The street was again of cobblestone and this time the air was filled with loud noises of joy for everyone was happy and singing loudly their Hosannas! I saw garments of every color being thrown onto the street. Tears of joy on many faces were for this MAN, Jesus. They knew He did miracles. They saw Him heal the sick, lame, blind and return the dead ~ to life. He was coming!

Suddenly an enormous shout went up that was almost deafening.

HOSANNA!
  HOSANNA!
    HOSANNA!

THERE HE IS!
  HE IS COMING!
    LOOK! HE IS HERE!

I stood on the sidelines as a stately, dignified Man passed by me on a diminutive donkey. I continued to watch as the donkey plodded along, stepping upon the many garments and palm branches that were now lying on the street. The crowd had pressed in upon Jesus but He still made His way slowly through them, touching people as He passed by. Several times He stopped to talk to someone and other times He stopped to touch and smile at a small child.

I watched with much interest as the procession went on into the city, until the crowd, noise, donkey and Jesus could no longer be seen. I stood absorbing the emotions of the air about me. I awakened to the beginning of my week, knowing my fears, but confident that whatever happened I would never be alone. Never ever again!

The Lord had instructed me to join the Presbyterian Church where Jim had been so kind in helping me throughout this spiritual experience and to become a member on Palm Sunday. I did and it was a truly wonderful experience and day!

My resignation was submitted to the Post Master, George . My last day to work was Good Friday. I now only had the future to look forward to with much anticipation and joy and did so, no matter what was to come!

30

+ Monday, Tuesday, Wednesday +

"The stone which the builders rejected
has become the head of the corner."

Psalm 118:22

In another dream, I was able to see men and women in the Temple area. They were milling around laughing and talking. Some were buying animals, white sheep and pigeons. Many pigeons. Several of the people looked to be very poor. I watched as Jesus walked through the area. He talked with some people in the lower area and then He walked to the upper area, where He could see the entire Temple yard area.

Suddenly, He reached out and overturned the tables and chairs that were nearest to Him. He then picked up money and threw it into the lower area. He pushed cages over and pigeons were flying everywhere. Animals and people were running everywhere and into each other. His voice loud and full of anger and despair, He cried out, "This House is being ruined by a den of thieves. Never again will this happen ~ never again!"

Amid all the chaos, Jesus then walked quietly toward a stairway, up the stairway, and disappeared through a doorway at its top.

On Tuesday, I spent much time in Bible study. I attended a local Lenten Service on Wednesday. After the service, I spent most of the night in study, pouring over the Scriptures to seek more answers and comfort. If the truth be known, I was actually seeking some added wisdom for the coming three days.

It was prayer that sustained me, both Jim's and my own during these days. And I shall never know the many from my church, family and friends who kept me in their prayers all those months. I am still grateful to this day for each and everyone of them.

31

+ Prayer Life +

Jesus said . . .
"Pray then like this:
Our Father who art in heaven,
Hallowed be thy name.
Thy kingdom come.
Thy will be done,
On earth as it is in heaven.
Give us this day our daily bread;
and forgive us our debts,
As we also have forgiven our debtors;
And lead us not into temptation,
But deliver us from evil."

Matthew 6:9-13

My prayer life became my strength throughout this conversion experience. From the very first day that I talked with Jim, prayer became the most important sharing for us. Jim gave prayers like these ears have never heard. Words were honest, sincere and elegantly pastoral. My prayers were so vastly different. Short, unsure, words - honest words, choppy and hesitant, but they were always said in utter sincerity.

My prayers were more like conversations for I spent a good part of the day talking to Him about everything and anything imaginable. I have continued this type of prayer because it is the best suited for me and it allows me to continue to have the closeness that I need to get through my day. It has never become a habit nor do I ever pray in rote. Even with the saying of The Lord's Prayer, each time I say it, I try to live each word, say each word as the Lord Himself must have said it to the disciples. Singing The Lord's Prayer as written by Malotte gives the words added depth, meaning and experience. My prayer conversations to me are always fresh and new for my life depends upon it more than anything else.

I have found that this type of continuing conversation with the Lord is my way of being myself. He is there in my deepest needs. I rely on Him in my life each and every moment. He has never failed me. I want the Lord to have a place in every part of my life, the little things as well as the big, the bad along with the good. For me, this kind of sharing gives me a closeness that I can depend upon in any situation.

He is with me...
      as I am sliding down an icy road,
      as I laugh at a silly joke.
      or is disappointed in me
...He is there...

my constant prayer conversations are our link.

+ Ultimate Love +

"And he took bread,
and when he had given thanks
he broke it and gave it to them,
saying,
"This is my body which is given for you.
Do this in remembrance of me."
And likewise the cup after supper, saying,
"This cup which is poured out for you is
the new covenant in my blood."

Luke 22:19-20

Another dream.

Once more I was a bystander, only this time I was in a room. It was quite large and more than adequately lit. I could see the whole room from my viewing place which was at the rear of the room. I was surprised by the horseplay and noise that were a part of the banquet scene. Several women were cooking and serving the food, although I noticed a heavy, tall man doing the overseeing of the meal. There seemed to be much laughing and backslapping among the men for the Passover Feast seemed to be one of an exceedingly happy nature. Out of the whole group of men only three or four seemed to understand the solemnity of the meal. To me, they looked like the same ones that I heard Jesus call by name by the Sea of Galilee when we had walked together in another dream. Even during the washing of the feet, there was much laughter and shouting. This scene disturbed me, but at the same time, I made an excuse for the men because I had the advantage of knowing what happened to each of them in their futures and also, I knew the total history of Jesus.

From the room, I followed Jesus as He walked along in the cool, quietness of the night and went into a garden. I was off in the distance, seeming to be on another knoll, but still I could see Jesus as He fell to the ground. His words to His beloved Father, "Abba, Father" were most earnest, and said in the utmost humility. The words were spoken with much emotion, yet were quiet words. His cried words, "Can't you take this cup from me?" made my soul cry. We didn't and don't understand such a gift. . .I don't deserve such a gift.

The still of the night with only that awesome, quiet voice breaking its serenity continues to be with me. The night, with its stillness, impressed me as the same stillness that was there when He was born. The air felt charged with electricity, yet it was beautiful, peaceful and quiet. The night enveloped me even when He arose. I saw and heard as He went to Peter and asked him to stay awake. And Peter, though he tried, could not. I realize that James and John were present in the Scriptural account, they played no role in my vision.

And then the guards came to get Him. It was far from a pleasant scene. So much shouting, and then I saw Peter running with the others out into the darkness. The guards seized Him, beating and dragging Him from the garden. In the court, and after His court appearance, the beatings continued – with fists and whippings with a lash. I saw Him standing. His head nobly bowed. He was gracefully silent. For me, it was the silence of someone who knew love for His enemies, and the forgiveness of such actions.

I saw then the crown forcefully placed upon His head –

Pain.   Pain.   More Pain!

Much physical pain.

One long very sharp thorn pierced Him in the center of the forehead. The blood spurted and started to trickle down past the right eye onto His cheek. His anguish I felt, not knowing how he could accept and stand firm yet endure and tolerate so much pain. I could feel the silent sound of His heart breaking, not – I am sure – because of His physical punishment but because of His acceptance of ALL THE SINS of humanity into His life and Spirit.

He withstood all of this pain in silence and I utterly agree with the centurion, "He could not have done it except He surely was THE SON OF GOD."
Luke 23:47

The fast that I had undertaken earlier gave me support to endure my knowledge of, and living through these most tragic and bittersweet events.

33

+ The Earthly End +

"When Jesus had received the vinegar,
he said,
"It is finished";
and
he bowed his head and
gave up his spirit."

John 19:30

And the dream continued. . .

And slowly, I followed as He went up to Golgotha. He staggered, He fell. The skin on His back was in shreds, the perspiration running into the open wounds. Help came on the way, for the weighted burden was lifted by another. The carrying of the cross to a hole dug in the earth, the foot of the cross, was for me sadness personified, as deeply as I could ever know it. Then the cross was dropped into the hole and the pain of the sudden slamming of the body tight against the nails in the hands and feet, is indescribable. It sears my soul to remember the pain. What did this innocent MAN do to deserve this?

The blood, the wound in His side, ran down His leg, over the foot and quite violently splashed upon the earth. Suddenly, the earth, receiving His blood, ripped itself open trying to repel what was being thrust upon it, and then the blood began to run in a river down the mountainside. The earth, and all of creation, shuddered. The river of blood ran on and on, becoming redder and more wide, moving very swiftly down toward the city. Suddenly it stopped. Silence and stillness was on and over the earth.

And I waited for Him to die. It seemed an eternity. More than a life time. His head bowed for the very last time.

He died.

He died.

The whole of earth and the sky was now in blackness and it was very BLACK!

As I looked upward, the lightning bolt flashed and hurled itself jagged across the sky but even with its light, it left the earth in stark. . .black. The crash of the thunder, for a fleeting second, removed the feeling of death. But then the earth

80

trembled beneath my feet as if it wanted to tear itself apart. The earth was wanting to reject the treasure of red that had just been poured into it. The very essence of nature was trying to reject what another part of the creation had done to the Creator's Son.

Just as suddenly, quiet came once again. It was not the quiet, peaceful, still of the birth or the garden scene, but a quietness that occurs after a storm, anticipating a better time to come.

As this scene left me, I was left in a black state of mind and emotion. The color came upon me in a depth beyond my wisdom to know.

Then came my last day of work. As I left the office, I walked to the church on a sunny, but cold afternoon. I enjoyed the walk, I felt I was walking into a freedom I had never known. I would miss my work at the post office, my co-workers, my customers, the sorting of letters, and the work at the counter. But, as I walked, I thought about new life and a new part of my life's journey. I looked forward to Tuesday and my trip to the University of Pittsburgh.

I found the church open and walked into the sanctuary a few minutes after noon. I sat very still thinking. Jim heard me come in and came and sat with me for a few minutes. We talked of 'cabbages and kings' which we considered small talk that we used when I needed to have a diversion from the sober mindedness and depth of my experience. We then talked about death. About one death, that of our Lord. . .the death of Jesus Christ, our Messiah.

I left the sanctuary, walking out into the cold sunny afternoon. I went home to ponder for myself the meaning of such a death for me. Indeed, was I worthy of such a death? Is anyone?

I traveled once more through my experiences of the past months, thinking about the people I knew who supported me, the absolute sustaining of me by my family, the church session who gave me their support and prayers, both the teachings and experiences by the Holy Spirit, Jim who stood by me, and especially and foremost, the Jesus that I now knew, both THE MAN AND THE SAVIOR. I also thought about the glorious honor that THE MAN had bestowed upon me. Why? It had all come to this BLACK end this day. What was to come next? What more would there be?

I was in for a surprise and another experience. I was to have a new understanding about death ~ and life!

34

+ Saturday +

"When I saw him, I fell at his feet as though dead.
But he laid his right hand upon me, saying,
'Fear not, I am the first and the last,
and the living one;
I died,
and behold
I am alive for evermore,
and I have the keys of Death and Hades."

Revelation 1:17-18

Saturday, I found myself once again in the sanctuary. I sat in my usual place, looking upon by now a very familiar white wooden cross which sits upon the communion table. My mind was still in a black state.

I was to embark upon another most painful experience.

My instruction was to sit quietly, which I did. The Lord said, "I will be with you. I want you to experience Hell."

I can only describe the experience as being in a total, pure, black area of endless space. The space had no side, no down, no up, no back, no front. It didn't matter if my eyes were closed or open, I found myself in a weightless condition, feeling as the astronauts must have felt in outer space but I was not tied to anything by a cord. In Hell, I had no connection to anything except the voice of Jesus. I felt like I was inside a black space not knowing if I was up, down or sideways!

Jesus said, "This is Hell. NO light, NO God"..... "Let me know when you have had enough." I answered, "I will."

I stood the condition for about seven or eight minutes and said, "Lord, I have had enough." He then instructed me to go and talk with Jim. I went into his office and he wanted to know what had happened to me, telling from the look on my face that something extraordinary had happened. Once again we talked about cabbages and kings. I then gained my composure and was able to tell him what had happened. He agreed that Hell would be likened only to that kind of experience...it would be very black without the Light of the Lord in our lives, in our world, and in the universe.

I thought it impossible, but this experience caused me to cling to God through

Jesus Christ even more. I had been given the knowledge of the fullness of life even inside the color black.

I know that it was only the presence of the Lord's voice that caused me, in that black Hell, to have sanity, because - had He not already done that for me in and through my childhood, yes, into my adulthood? My journey through life, and in this intimate experience had led me from dark into light, back into dark and then into life again..

I had found the Light of Life!

My wondrous journey was over.

My reaction to what had happened was instructive. . .I had always wanted what I now owned! I wanted the Light and I wanted to cling to my new knowledge. I wanted to have the Lord in every part of my life and I reaffirmed this to Him. I wanted to remember forever Abraham, Moses. Samuel had also been called by voice in the middle of the night, called by name. I wanted to remember their journeys and the privilege I had of walking with Christ and that all their journeys had been part of my journey. I remembered the trust of Jim. I remember my promise to God. But mostly in my remembering, I remembered THE MAN who had died for me. I remembered THE MAN who gave me life. I remembered how much THE MAN loved me. Ultimately, death and Hell to me was only knowledge because The Trinity made it only knowledge.

Rethinking the experiences of the day, I found it difficult to sleep that night.

35

+ The Hallelujah Chorus +

"Then the seventh angel blew his trumpet,
and there were loud voices in heaven, saying,
'The kingdom of the world has become
the kingdom of our Lord
and of his Christ,
and he shall reign for ever and ever.'"

Revelation 11:15

About 2:00 AM, I found myself looking into my bathroom mirror. I stared at, and even studied my own face, which now seemed to me to be the face of a stranger. I also studied my eyes. Did I really have such an adventure? How few on this earth have ever had such an awesome opportunity and experience. And now I felt so much strength that I was ready, eager really, to change my life.

My reaction?

YES!
YES!
YES!
I am ready Lord!!!

I know and have no doubts, the Lord will be with me. In just a few hours, we will be celebrating once again His resurrection.

HE LIVES!

HE LIVES!

My JESUS CHRIST LIVES!

My heart began to overflow with joy at this knowledge and suddenly, gloriously, into my head came a chorus of many many perfectly blended voices singing the words to Handel's Messiah of the Hallelujah Chorus. I wondered as I listened, even singing along – words remembered from my high school choral time. I wondered if the whole world was hearing what I was hearing, for surely it was loud enough!

I smiled, grinned and laughed through many tears of joy.

Tomorrow would be the last day of this particular part of my extraordinary journey in life.

36

+ A New Beginning +

*" For I know that my Redeemer lives,
and at last he will stand upon the earth;"*

Job 19:25

Sunrise on my first day. Easter day. A perfect day following a perfect night. A perfectly miserable day weather wise, snowy, rainy, cold and windy, but a perfect day nevertheless. And yet, as the morning wore on the sun came out to warm us.

Easter service and a day for joining church.

I believe ~

I believe in the Messiah.
I believe in THE MAN called Jesus of Nazareth.
I believe in THE MAN CALLED Christ.
I believe in THE MAN called Son of God.

I have become a member of the kingdom that is so near at hand.

I found the reaffirmation of self. A self that is worth everything, at least to THE MAN. Thoughts of victory over death, what is death that I should fear it? Death is a step into eternity, into forever. I look toward it with great anticipation, eagerness, knowing:

The Creator and the Creation
The fullness of eternity
Its perfection
Its peace
Death is not an end
Death is a beginning into forever
Forever is with God and His Son

Such love. . .

TOMORROWS

Jesus said
". . .therefore I tell you,
do not be anxious about your life,
what you shall eat,
nor about your body,
what you shall put on.
For life is more than food,
and the body more than clothing. . ."

Luke 12:22a-23

It was a most glorious, grand, worshipful Sunday!
On Monday I found a day of excitement and anticipation.
Tuesday found me on the highway headed to my long awaited superior education. As I drove, I asked myself, "Could anything I learn at Pitt, be as fruitful as what I had already learned in the last five months? Could it? Nothing will ever be as astounding a ton of knowledge than knowing ~ ~ ~

God IS!

Jesus IS!

The Holy Spirit IS!

The Lord bid me to accomplish my education in six years, and so my tomorrows became filled with the excitement and challenges of studies and more studies. I began as a student at the University of Pittsburgh, June, 1974 and graduated April, 1977 with a Bachelor Degree in Political Science. I entered Pittsburgh Theological Seminary, September, 1977 and graduated May, 1980 with a Master of Divinity degree. In those six years, I also completed two Clinical Pastoral Education Programs, one in a prison and the other in a state mental hospital. I was ordained by Beaver-Butler Presbytery on November 22, 1980 and called to be the Stated Supply pastor of two churches in the Presbytery. From those wonderful churches, I felt my call to become an Intentional Interim Minister for the Presbyterian Church, USA . I served in twenty one churches in twelve states.

In 1995, I received my Doctor of Ministry degree, also from Pittsburgh Theological Seminary. All of my formal education, the many special professors, the education that I acquired with the various types of persons that I met in that time, gave me a well-rounded education, plus the bonus of many new friends, new sisters and brothers in Christ.

And my Christ and His promise.

"Peace I leave with you;
my peace I give to you:
not as the world gives do I give to you.
Let not your hearts be troubled,
neither let them be afraid."

John 14:27

I claim that my Chronicle is not unique. All who follow the Prince of Peace find fulfillment in their lives. My journey is perhaps different from others but like all other journeys with the Lord, it is not complete. Every day brings new growth because of new experiences. Meeting Jesus Christ has given me life, and I enjoy living and I try mightily to live one day at a time. I am most grateful to God for my gift of life, its fullness, its knowledge, its love and for my good health. I look back over my life in the full realization that God cared for me as a small child, protected me and kept me sane in my feelings of rejection, and I know that God, Jesus Christ and the Holy Spirit still cares for me this same way today. As they care for each and every person on the face of God's creation – this earth we were given!

God 'THE MAN' gave me individual worth. This came at great cost to Him. The cost? The life of His Son, Jesus. But even in His death, Jesus Christ became more alive than when He had physically lived and walked among us.

I believe in the resurrection power of His death because after some two thousand years, its power still gave life in abundance to me! I live this moment only because HE LIVES.

I ask you, I tell you, if you do not have this kind of love, caring and fulfillment in your life, if "you know him not" ~ invite Him into your heart and life! Give yourself the gift of life and worth. Accept life in abundance, THIS DAY, THIS HOUR, THIS MOMENT, THIS SECOND!

"So if the Son makes you free, you will be free indeed."

John 8:36

And an eternal promise from Christ ~

"Peace I leave with you; my peace I give to you:
not as the world gives do I give to you.
Let not your hearts be troubled,
neither let them be afraid."

John 14:27

Reflection

Did you think . . .
Did you see . . .
Did you remember . . .

Jesus in Gethsemane
    where He shed tears for all people
        for you   for me
HE   perfect but arrested
    denied in the hearts of most
HE   was tried with a sentence predetermined
    a court fixed with hatred
HIS punishment – stripped and beaten
        a whip of glass, bones, metal
          HIS back, flesh hanging
             blood running
          HIS chest, naked
             sweaty
              A punishment undeserved . . .

HE carried a cross
    rough and burning into a shoulder scourged
    the crown upon His head
    piercing the skin – more bleeding – more pain
            He staggered up the cobblestone way

HE fell to one knee
    where you stand watching
HE looks at our
    pain and agony etching His face
        eyes that searched your depths
          eyes of blue green gray
            eyes filled with pain sorrow pleading
               yet love and
               peace

a voice that sears you – heart and soul
        will you do My will and follow Me?
      you deny those eyes
    you try
  and cannot will not do not
you trust those eyes that voice
        forever . . .

you follow
     up the hill
you watch as the cross plunges into a hole in the earth
     HE groans and your soul cries
         and you wait
              wait for the innocent to die
              wait for the earth to run red
              wait for the sky to blacken
              wait for the earth to shudder
        hell and silence for three days . . .

DAWN

    the most beautiful sunrise ever
        the first Easter morn
           the trumpets announce
              the triumphant cry heard for centuries

Hallelujah . . . HE IS RISEN!!! HE LIVES!!!

JOY beyond compare
         and peace
HE died for us to live
        with HIM through all eternity

           do you reflect . . .
              do you even pause . . .

THANK YOU GOD! For loving us so much.

Printed in the United States
By Bookmasters